C000138902

AFTERSIGHT

AND

FORESIGHT

AFTERSIGHT
AND
FORESIGHT

The gifts reserved for age

by

Denis Hunter

Denis Hunter, a retired Salvation Army officer, lives in Blackheath, South London. Now in his 88th year, he was commissioned and ordained from the William Booth College, London, in 1938.

Pauline, 'his continual comrade in the War' was Promoted to Glory on 3 September 2002, three days after their diamond wedding celebration.

By the same authors
(*Denis and Pauline Hunter)

* *While the light lingers* 2005
* *A very gracious lady* 2003
Paul Hunter   2001
Centuries of faith   2000
Christus Victor   1997
Bright Ring of Words   1990
(edited by Pauline for Colonel Arthur Smith)

FOR PAULINE
forever with the Lord

with a retirement salute to
John Gowans (General, 1999-2002) and
John Larsson (General, 2002-2006)
gifted leaders and trusted friends

Since our concern was speech, and speech impelled us
To purify the dialect of the tribe
And urge the mind to aftersight and foresight,
Let me disclose the gifts reserved for age
To set a crown upon your lifetime's effort.

T.S. Eliot
Four Quartets

First published in 2006 by
Denis Hunter
in cooperation with
The Salvation Army
UK Territory Literary Unit
101 Newington Causeway, London SE1 6BN

ISBN: 0 85412 751 8

Distributed by SP&S Ltd
1 Tiverton Street
London SE1 6NT

[44] (0) 20 7367 6570

Printed by Proprint
Riverside Cottages
Old Great North Road
Stibbington
Cambridgeshire
PE8 6LR

[44] (0) 1733 371825

Cover Design — Berni Georges

CONTENTS

While their origin is nowhere stated,

the roots of

The Salvation Army Articles of Faith

are clearly in the Wesleyan tradition.

The Articles bear a striking similarity

in words and content to

Methodist New Connexion doctrines

which can be traced back to at least 1838.

William Booth was an Ordained Minister

of the Methodist New Connexion.

Salvation Story

Doctrine is the teaching of the church. It is an expanded explanation of faith, founded on Scripture and developed from a basic creed. The (Salvation Army's) eleven Articles of Faith are an expression both of personal faith and of a common vision.

General Paul. A. Rader (R)

SALVATION ARMY DOCTRINES

As set out in Schedule 1 of The Salvation Army Act, 1980

We believe that the Scriptures of the Old and New Testaments were given by inspiration of God; and that they only constitute the Divine rule of Christian faith and practice.

We believe that there is only one God, who is infinitely perfect, the Creator, Preserver and Governor of all things, and who is the only proper object of religious worship.

We believe that there are three persons in the Godhead – the Father, the Son and the Holy Ghost, undivided in essence and co-equal in power and glory.

We believe that in the person of Jesus Christ the Divine and human natures are united, so that He is truly and properly God and truly and properly man.

We believe that our first parents were created in a state of innocency, but by their disobedience they lost their purity and happiness; and that in consequence of their fall all men have become sinners, totally depraved, and as such are justly exposed to the wrath of God.

We believe that the Lord Jesus Christ has by His suffering and death made an atonement for the whole world so that whosoever will may be saved.

We believe that repentance towards God, faith in our Lord Jesus Christ and regeneration by the Holy Spirit are necessary to salvation.

We believe that we are justified by grace, through faith in our Lord Jesus Christ; and that he that believeth hath the witness in himself.

We believe that continuance in a state of salvation depends upon continued obedient faith in Christ.

We believe that it is the privilege of all believers to be wholly sanctified, and that their whole spirit and soul and body may be preserved blameless unto the coming of our Lord Jesus Christ.

We believe in the immortality of the soul; in the resurrection of the body; in the general judgement at the end of the world; in the eternal happiness of the righteous and in the endless punishment of the wicked.

INTRODUCTION

General Dr A. Shaw Clifton, LL B, BD, PhD, AKC
and Commissioner Helen Clifton, BA, PGCE.

GENERAL CLIFTON took command of The Salvation Army on Sunday, 2 April 2006, in succession to General John Larsson. Major Sally Storey, the heroine of *Aftersight and Foresight*, and Peter, the hero (anti-hero?) salute them both.

Sally and Peter also wholeheartedly greet Commissioners John and Elizabeth Matear, newly appointed territorial leaders. The good Lord continues to provide the Army with godly and splendidly equipped international and national leaders.

On the evening of Thursday, 8 July 2005, the General, at that time Territorial Commander for the UK and Republic of Ireland Territory, presented a lecture in the William Booth College Assembly Hall to some 200 Salvationists and friends.

The subject of the lecture was 'A Thinking Salvationist', commemorating to the day 75 years of officer training at the College. In his challenging 50-minute address he spoke of the importance of Army history:

> I do not think anyone can rightly claim to be a thinking Salvationist without a knowledge of Army history. Unless we know where we have come from we cannot know who we are today. Unless we have insights into the gracious ways of God with us in the past, we cannot have clear vision for today and tomorrow. A thinking Salvationist has a knowledge of our history, so that she or he can think intelligently and in context about the present and the future ...

> It is even more important that we have *godly*, thinking Salvationists, those who know the blessing of a clean heart.

Peter was surely a fly on the wall on that July evening.

WITH MANY THANKS...

You are old, Father William, the young man cried.
The few locks which are left you are grey
Robert Southey's young man might have continued:
If you seriously purpose to write a new book
You'll need lots of help, I would say.

That help has been forthcoming in generous measure:

Major David Dalziel, Literary Editor at Territorial Headquarters, has provided professional know-how, with the back-up throughout of Major Christine Clement, Editor-in-chief.

Major Charles King and designer Berni Georges have produced the eye-catching cover.

The sleuths at the Army's Heritage Centre at William Booth College have been hot on every trail suggested by any clue given to them — including Major Stephen Grinsted, Director; Gordon Taylor, Archivist and Beccy Hine, Researcher.

Permission to feature the old Clapton Congress Hall in association with the new Clapton Portico was given immediately by Brady and Mallalieu, Architects. I thank them.

Major David Shakespeare, Business Services Director, William Booth College, veteran Colonel Brindley Boon, Colonel Gordon Becker, Salvationist Morvyn Finch, of Woodbridge Corps, Lieut-Colonel Stephen Pallant and Major David Pickard have also revealed 'an infinite capacity for taking pains' on my behalf.

The contributions of Commissioner John Swinfen and Lieut-Colonel Miriam Frederiksen, each essay totally distinct from the other, are choice indeed. Major John Wainwright, Secretary for Business Administration, THQ, gave immediate permission for staff members Susan Scott and Mandy Miller to tackle the original handwritten manuscript. They did so with gratifying speed. I am grateful also to the many comrades and friends of the years who have slipped unannounced into and out of the narrative from time to time.

Robert Southey, Poet Laureate, might have concluded *The Old Man's Comforts, And How He Gained Them* with:
Our pleasure in meeting with Sally and Pete
Is quite clear, and your book is complete.

SYNOPSIS

PETER, a man in his fifties, had been a member of the local Salvation Army band in earlier years. The death of his wife has created a vacuum in his life. His children have all flown the nest. He needs friendship. Looking back to his younger years he 'slips in' to the corps meeting hall one Sunday morning and is greeted warmly. He feels at ease immediately.

This first visit, after so many years absence, is followed by many more. Peter becomes a regular worshipper. One Sunday morning, he responds to Major Sally Storey's Bible message and goes forward to kneel at the Mercy Seat. Peter has come home to the Lord and to the Army.

Major Sally Storey, the corps officer, encourages Peter to go on with the Lord. She does this in a number of one-to-one conversations. To encourage his re-orientation back into Salvation Army life, she arranges to meet him at various Salvation Army centres in London. Peter, who has taken early retirement, finds that he looks forward to these interesting Army visits.

Some weeks after Peter's mercy-seat response the Major gives him a copy of the articles of war to read. He vaguely remembers signing these a number of years earlier. They will call for careful reading, because he has totally forgotten them. Whenever Peter and the Major meet he is ready to bombard her with questions – what does this word mean, or that phrase?

Aftersight and Foresight is a record of some of these conversations. If both Peter and Sally seem to possess knowledge beyond their years from time to time — The Gifts reserved for Age — the author pleads literary licence.

Aftersight and Foresight may also be thought of as a play for broadcasting
(on Radio Salvo with a friendly narrator as guide!).

1

On Location
in Chatham Dockyard
Saved!

WHEN THE newly appointed chaplain joined HMS Winchelsea during World War II he was intrigued to discover a Salvation Army bonnet hanging in the wardroom. Some months before, Winchelsea had rescued a torpedoed seaman from the waters of the North Atlantic. Winchelsea eventually made port and the rescued seaman happily made his way home. Full of gratitude to his rescuers he wondered how he might thank them appropriately. What symbol might be a suitable acknowledgement? The crew of Winchelsea had saved his life.

He visited his local Salvation Army corps, secured a Salvation Army bonnet, boxed and posted it to Winchelsea's Captain.

Winchelsea's chaplain eventually became chaplain on HMS Ark Royal. He recounted his Winchelsea story to the officer of the Devonport Morice Town Salvation Army Corps when the corps band presented a service of carols on board HMS Ark Royal, Christmas 1956. The dockyard at Chatham has long since been mothballed, but it remains open to tourists.

The chaplain did not state the name of any port— Rothesay? Plymouth? Liverpool? — Chatham, Kent, a mere handful of miles for Sally and Peter to travel, seemed as likely a location as any other.

Aftersight and Foresight (1)

We believe that repentance towards God, faith in our Lord Jesus Christ, and regeneration by the Holy Spirit are necessary to salvation …

Doctrine 7

SALLY: You came to the Mercy Seat, Peter

Peter: It seemed the right thing to do and I wanted to do it. I need the Lord in the centre of my life again. Your sermon did the trick.

Sally: Message, Peter, not sermon. Salvation Army officers don't preach sermons, or should not try to do so. Chief of the Staff Bramwell Booth wrote in 1881 'the days of ordinary sermonising are passed away for ever with us'.

Peter: 'Believe in the Lord Jesus Christ and you will be saved'[1], you said — and the vocal solo by that songster got hold of me, too.

Sally: (sings softly)

    He's the Christ of the human road,
    And he offers to carry our load,
  He's walking our way, ev'ry night ev'ry day,
    This Christ of the human road.
  He is human and yet so divine,
  And he knows your heart's sorrow, and mine.
  In all times of need he's a true friend indeed,
    This Christ of the human road

(George Bennard)

Peter: You have a beautiful voice too, Major.

Sally: We were all praying for you as you sought the Lord.

Peter: I want to go on with the Lord, Major.

---

[1] Acts 16:31

Sally: St Paul teaches that you are now 'in Christ' [2], a branch grafted on to the living vine[3].

Peter: Yes, I do want to go on with the Lord.

Sally: Personal prayer will help you Peter. Do you jog?

Peter: Every lunchtime.

Sally: Prayer-jog, Peter, like Major Margaret Yuill does.

Peter: How does she manage that?

Sally: Prayer is more than:

> God bless me and my wife,
> Our Jack and his wife,
> Us four and no more!

When Major Margaret jogs[4] she has a clear framework of prayer in her mind. First, thanksgiving to God for who he is, then thanks for life itself, then for her new life in Christ. Then she prays in the spirit of contrition, 'create in me a clean heart, O God[5]', then she gives thanks for her birth family — her parents, and for her own daughters and husband. Finally she prays for the coming of God's Kingdom.

Peter: How wonderful it is to jog with God.

Sally: Along the road where holy men have jogged![6] And it's a marathon, not a sprint, gum boots sometimes, not always running shoes, Peter

Peter: Am I saved? I am, aren't I?

Sally: You were saved at around three in the afternoon of the first Good Friday. When you came to the Lord at the Mercy Seat you entered into your inheritance.

Peter: But isn't 'being saved' 'old hat' ?

---

[2] 2 Corinthians. 5:17

[3] John 15:5

[4] *Salvationist* 24 September 2005

[5] Psalm 51:10

[6] *SASB* 583

Sally: Glory to Jesus I am nicely saved,
(sings softly) My many, many, many sins are all forgiven,
My name is entered in the sacred book of heaven,
Glory to Jesus. I am nicely saved,
Sing it out! Ring it out! Nicely saved! [7]
(Kristian M. Fristrup)

Peter: As I say — a pleasant ditty, but old hat.

Sally: Hold on! Last July, Stapleford Corps opened a charity shop in their part of Nottingham, its brand reads:

NICELY SAVED
NEW TO YOU SHOP

Two Mayors were present at the opening ceremony, local clergy and other dignitaries also. And what do you think Stapleford Band played as its musical contribution?

Peter: Tell me …

Sally: 'Nicely saved', a march written by Lieut-Colonel Ray Steadman-Allen when he was just a Captain, based on Staff-Captain Fristrup's earlier melody.

Peter: Steadman-Allen? I remember that name. Nothing old hat in the new charity shop in Stapleford! Nicely saved!

Sally: All proceeds fund a nearby Salvation Army Drop-In Youth Centre. Yes, Peter, you are saved. 'If we confess our sins, God is faithful and just to forgive us our sins and to cleanse us from all unrighteousness'[8].

Peter: I believe it with all my heart.

Sally: You will make a splendid Salvationist once again, Peter. Do you think you could find time to read this? [9]

---

[7] See illustration p.6   [9] See illustration on back cover
[8] 1 John 1:9

Peter: What is this you are giving me?

Sally: The Salvationist's articles of war. All Salvationists sign this covenant at the time of their enrolment and we all hope you will do so again.

Peter: It looks a formidable document. No shortage of words. I remember it vaguely from years ago.

Sally: The articles of war fall into two parts:

1. What a Salvationist believes (our eleven doctrines)

2. What a Salvationist promises (our bond of agreement)

— a soldier's covenant.

Peter: And I sign this?

Sally: Not now. Take it away and read it carefully.

Peter: I'll do that Major, thank you.

Sally: Good night, Peter. Go on with the Lord, and don't forget to prayer-jog!

On Location
at London Gatwick Airport
Not Set in Concrete

ONCE AGAIN we travel south out of London, to Gatwick Airport, 30 miles out into Sussex. We found the Salvation Army chaplain, Lieut-Colonel Stephen Pallant in conversation with a group of 'meeters and greeters' in the South Terminal shopping mall. Stephen greeted us warmly, bade the group Godspeed and took us to the chaplain's office. Major Sally asked Stephen to outline a little of the Gatwick story for us.

History confirms that 750 years ago a certain John de Gatwick owned the land which eventually, in 1958, became London Gatwick Airport, built at a cost of £7.8 million. A second terminal was opened 30 years later, in 1988, costing £200 million! Today Gatwick is the busiest single runway airport in the world, handling more than 32 million passengers annually. Its work force numbers 30,000.

Teams of chaplains minister in large and small airports throughout the world. At Gatwick Lieut-Colonel Stephen Pallant and Major Robin McIntosh work with Church of England and Roman Catholic chaplains serving the airport community as they reach out to all members of staff, passengers and visitors. An airport chaplain probably contacts, speaks with and ministers to more people in one day than most clergy do in a whole week!

Worship is at the heart of a chaplain's day, whether it takes the form of a Roman Catholic Mass, Anglican Holy Communion or a Free Church Service.

Airport Chaplaincy is front-line evangelism; a visible presence. (The Salvation Army thrives on visibility: communicating, responding, informing and 'loitering with intent'). Our work consists of priestly, pastoral and prophetic ministry to and with people who work at and use the Airports.

Stephen Pallant, Lieut-Colonel

Aftersight and Foresight (2)

The earliest Christians acknowledged one another in
the simple confession 'Jesus is Lord' (1 Corinthians 12:3).
This was their creed ...

Salvation Story

SALLY: How are you finding the articles of war Peter?

Peter: It's a sizeable document, right enough, Major.
Am I allowed to ask questions?

Sally: Go ahead! All Salvationists sign the articles of war

Peter: Some of the language seems a little dated.

Sally: You mean part two — a Soldier's Covenant, the promises
we make?

Peter: No problem with part two. I don't drink, tobacco is a
menace, I don't womanise, I am not in debt and I don't
use drugs.

Sally: The doctrines?

Peter: Isn't some of the language a little antiquated, for instance
'God is the only proper object of religious worship'.
God a 'proper object' ?

Sally: Basically they are the doctrines of the Methodist New
Connexion of 1838. William Booth adopted them for
his Christian Mission.

Peter: 1838 language for the 21st century? Isn't that rather
like a political party going to the country with the slogan,
'Magna Carta or bust, Magna Carta for ever' ?

Sally: The historic creeds are recited in Anglican churches
every Sunday.

Peter: But an Anglican is not asked to sign up to the church's
historic 39 articles, dubbed by some the 40 stripes save

one. Truth is not best expressed in outmoded vocabulary. Think of the 'wicked' way that wicked has changed its meaning!

Sally: Words can change colour with the passage of time, I agree, so what do you propose?

Peter: No proposals Major, just thinking aloud. Remember, you agreed I could ask questions.

Sally: Every discipline has its own special language. Religion is no exception.

Peter: But to simplify is to clarify and to abbreviate is to strengthen.

Sally: But I don't analyse like that. If I were to say to my people 'I don't believe this or that', it would confuse them. I love my work and my people.

Peter: Eliminate the negative, accentuate the positive, Major, but do you need eleven doctrines? Some seem to duplicate, or certainly to overlap; two with three; three, four and six seem to belong together; three with seven; eight with nine.

Sally: Re-writing the script Peter? Aaron advising Moses?

Peter: Ideas command, Major. Too many words can confuse. Did you say that there have been amendments to the doctrines from time to time?

Sally: The Methodist New Connexion of 1838 affirmed twelve Articles of Faith. Booth's East London Christian Revival Society affirmed seven doctrines closely related to these.

Peter: And the Revival Society became The Christian Mission?

Sally: As far as I understand it, the first General Conference of the Christian Mission in 1870 slightly amended Doctrine 1 then expanded Doctrine 2 to form Doctrines 2 and 3. Doctrine 3 was renumbered 4; Doctrine 4 was revised and renumbered 5; Doctrine 5 became 6; Doctrine 6 was renumbered 7; new Doctrines 8 and 9 were added and

Doctrine 7 was re-numbered 10. Later, the 'Rules of The Christian Mission' [1873/4] added a new Doctrine 9, and Doctrines 9 and 10 from the 1870 version were renumbered 10 and 11.

In the Mission's Deed Poll, 1875, the last phrase of Doctrine 3 was moved to the end of Doctrine 2, and the 11 Articles of Faith took the form we still use today.

Peter: Phew! So the doctrines as worded are not set in stone?

Sally: The Christian Mission Conference of 1876 added a postscript to Doctrines 9 and 10 — 'The Roots of Bitterness' paragraph. This was subsequently included in full or in part in various editions of 'The Doctrines of The Salvation Army'; in *The Handbook of Doctrine* and in the articles of war.

Peter: So changes have been made from time to time?

Sally: That additional paragraph was not included in the 1878 Deed Poll nor does it appear in the 1980 Act.

Peter: There you are, you see. Not set in concrete.

Sally: But any further change would take for ever. More than one General in recent years has seen the need for rewording but has not had time to address the task. *Salvation Story* explains the text but makes no attempt to revise it.

Peter: Would the General need to consult Parliament if he wished to make adjustments?

Sally: No, the Doctrines form Schedule 1 of the 1980 Act. He could make any changes he felt necessary, but he would need the written agreement of more than two thirds of Commissioners on active service.

Peter: And countless thousands of Salvationists have accepted the Doctrines as they now stand. I see the problem.

Sally: And the Doctrines are included, or at least referred to in the constitution of the Army in every country where the flag flies.

Peter: I am not surprised that Generals have hesitated.

Sally: As a matter of interest Peter, what alterations would you wish to see. What is causing your hesitation?

Peter: Not so much alterations as definitions Major.

Sally: Are you seriously intending to become a Salvationist?

Peter: Indeed I am. I think the Army is an amazing church. How many churches does a town need?

Sally: How many oases does a desert need? But, Peter, we are a mission, not a church — a river of grace flowing into the community.

Peter: And I can accept the International Mission Statement without a moment's hesitation:

> The Salvation Army, an International Movement, is an evangelical part of the universal Church. Its message is based on the Bible, its ministry is motivated by love for God, its mission is to preach the Gospel of Jesus Christ and meet human needs in His name without discrimination.

> Yes, I go for that. I would like to sign up to that, no hesitation.

Sally: So we are talking about definitions in the Doctrines, possible revisions of language here and there?

Peter: Yes, basically, although I have to say that I have serious problems with one or two of your … er, our beliefs.

Sally: Such as?

Peter: For instance, is God really in charge of the world and is the whole of the Bible inspired by Him and, quite the most difficult of all for me, is God really going to pronounce everlasting punishment on people who don't believe in Him?

Sally: One at a time, Peter — Ah! There's the airport intercom announcing prayers. Let's go into the chapel.

11

On Location
at the Newly Rebuilt IHQ
Was God in the Tsunami?

THE VISITS to Chatham Dockyard and to Gatwick Airport were made by road, car-parking not a problem at either place. Parking in Queen Victoria Street, in the heart of the city of London is a different story.

The Major rendezvoused with Peter at Blackheath, south London, railway station, travelling to Blackfriars Station, a journey of some 17 minutes. A short walk towards Mansion House tube station brought them to International Headquarters, at the head of the Millennium Bridge.

International Headquarters at 101 Queen Victoria Street, London stands no further than a drumbeat from St. Paul's Cathedral.

'101' has been the centre of the Army's world-embracing mission since 1881. Removal from 227 Whitechapel Road, an old dwelling house, involved two trips in a fruiterer's horse-drawn van plus a handcart. Halfway to the new city offices one of the wheels fell off the handcart. Cadet William Whattam attempted to fix it, while his colleague, known as 'Zulu George', held off the roughs by threatening them with the flagpole that formed part of the precious cargo. The rest of the journey was made on one wheel with one perspiring cadet pushing and the other holding the handcart on the wheel-less side.

Robert Sandall,
The History of The Salvation Army, Vol II, p. 208

 Aftersight and Foresight (3)

We believe that there is only one God who is infinitely perfect, the Creator, Preserver and Governor of all things, and who is the only proper object of religious worship

Doctrine 2

PETER: This is a remarkable building, Major, thank you for bringing me here.

Sally: Declared open in the presence of Her Royal Highness, the Princess Royal, on 9 November 2004.

Peter: The Army's own Crystal Palace, a totally glass structure.

Sally: Modern in design, frugal in operation, evangelical in purpose! It is a success story, both architecturally and financially. It 'wows' the city.

The Journal *Property Week* of 5 November 2004 reported:

> A canny deal has given The Salvation Army a brand new headquarters in the heart of London, free of charge. It is the kind of property deal that most occupiers dream about. First, an owner-occupier drastically reduces the amount of space it needs, then it sells a long lease on the space it has vacated to a developer for £15.4 million. The developer transforms the entire site into modern offices. The money raised from the sale of the lease funds the construction of a new headquarters on the same site for the owner-occupier.
>
> The developer also agrees to pay ground-rent to the original occupier which remains the freeholder, providing a minimum of £200,000 a year in extra income .... The Salvation Army may be a charitable Christian organisation but it is not naïve when it comes to making property deals as the partners who worked with it will testify.

Peter: There are astute heads on the shoulders of your Army leaders, Major. George Bernard Shaw defined genius as the ability to see a target which other people could not see, to aim at it and to hit it. Who was your William Tell?

Sally: General John Gowans, now retired. He inspired his top IHQ team with his vision. The late Commr Brian Taylor, International Secretary for Business at the time, gave exact adjustment to all the nuts and bolts.

This also reminds me that many years ago Major Andy Miller (now Commissioner, retired) was responsible for Salvation Army fund-raising in the city of Chicago.

Big money was needed for a major capital development to make possible an extension of our work among alcoholic men and women — an ever-increasing social problem. What campaign slogan might win a response in Chicago's boardrooms? To what kind of succinct appeal might hard-headed business men respond? Andy's appeal brochure, sent to chairmen and presidents of companies, read:

> **THE SALVATION ARMY REGRETS TO INFORM YOU THAT BUSINESS HAS NEVER BEEN BETTER.**

Peter: Is this restaurant open to the public?

Sally: Five days weekly although, of course, IHQ handles day-to-day business 24/7, allocating resources with strategic, long range planning. IHQ is a resource centre for the world-wide Army, a facilitator of ideas and policies. Twenty languages are used here daily, but 175 are used across the world. The first floor is the nerve centre. That's where the offices of the General and the Chief of the Staff are located. Australian-born Commissioner Robin Dunster is the first woman Chief of Staff to be appointed by any General.

Peter: Only one General?

Sally: His writ runs benevolently into the whole Salvation Army world. Each Army Territory is autonomous, answering to the General geographically through one of five international secretaries. A General retires from office on his 68th birthday or after five years as General, whichever comes first. He hits the ground running every morning.

Peter: So if the General is in charge of the whole Army world, then, is God really in charge?

Sally: That is a strange question Peter! Our second Doctrine states:
> We believe that there is only one God, who is infinitely perfect, the Creator, Preserver and Governor of all things and who is the only proper object of religious worship.

Peter: Proper object of religious worship? Isn't that an odd way of thinking about God? That needs up-dating for a start. What about the Tsunami? Where does your second Doctrine fit into the Tsunami or the other way round? Some people might say that God is the most frightful terrorist of them all!

15

Sally: You must not say things like that Peter.

Peter: What about Lord Attenborough?

Sally: The film producer? His Ghandi is unforgettable.

Peter: Attenborough lost a daughter, a granddaughter and his daughter's mother-in-law in the Tsunami. Would you come alongside him and say, 'Cheer up, old friend, God is the Creator, Governor, and Preserver of the universe'?

Sally: Ghandi is a powerful film.

Peter: And Hurricane Katrina? Did you see the TV shot of that wretched man in New Orleans moaning like a stricken animal; 'I've lost my wife, I can't find my wife!' What would you say to him — 'Cheer up, brother, this is God's world'?

Sally: Katrina brought total devastation to New Orleans.

Peter: And the North Pakistan earthquake?

Sally: 'God so loved the world that he gave his only begotten Son...'[1]

Peter: What about his forgotten sons and his three ugly daughters, Su, Kate and Irtha?

Sally: You mean Tsunami, Katrina, the Pakistan earthquake?

Peter: An ugly and an unholy trinity Major. If there were a tsunami in the English Channel and the Thames Barrier collapsed with the whole of Eastern England under water from Scarborough to Exeter, would you still want to tell us 'God is the Creator, Governor and Preserver of all things'?

Sally: Natural disasters present enormous problems for Christian faith.

Peter: You mean 'God's in His Heaven, all's right with the world' — and it isn't?

Sally: St. Paul teaches that creation is in a state of gestation slowly coming to full term.[2]

[1] John 3:16. [2] Romans 8:22:

16

Peter: That's for theologians, Major. Try telling that to the man in the pub!

Sally: God moves in a mysterious way his wonders to perform.

Peter: Please, please, don't say it, Major. Hundreds of thousands lie buried in mass graves in Indonesia.

Sally: I dare not think of it. What can any one individual do? The whole world rushed to succour the survivors of those three disasters. The Army played its part.[3]

Peter: I just ask, Major, that when you speak of the love of God in your meetings, somewhere in the back of your mind you are thinking, 'This is a hard saying for many people'. By the way, did you hear the Queen's broadcast to the Commonwealth last Christmas Day?

Sally: No, I was at the Christmas Day dinner for shut-ins at our hall.

Peter: That was compassion in action, Major — making good things happen for people unable to make them happen for themselves. The Queen said, 'This last year has reminded us that this world is not always an easy or a safe place to live in, but it is the only place we have.' That was realism right enough.

Sally: Here we are in this beautiful building with the sunshine streaming through and we are having these sad thoughts.

Peter: I do believe in God, Major, but how can I pen my name to the second Doctrine as it stands?

Sally: How would you describe God then?

Peter: The best I can manage at the moment is to affirm that all life comes from God and all life returns to him. I will need to wrestle with that second Doctrine's statement. It does not ring true.

Sally: There's General Clifton off on another demanding campaign … 'God bless you General!'

---

[3] See colour plates.

For many years Generals conducted a special day's meetings in London annually, along a chosen theme. Some 60 or so years ago the selected venue for the day was Westminster Chapel. The minister-emeritus of Westminster Chapel, Dr. Campbell Morgan, had been invited by the General to return to his old charge for the afternoon session to bring a message of greeting and goodwill. The great man responded gracefully when the General presented him to the congregation. He commended the day's theme then added: Of course, I am old enough to remember similar days conducted by your Founder. In those days every year would have the same title — 'A Day with God'. Indeed, I recall that some years would be announced 'Two Days with God' (he paused) — No, I'm wrong. The posters read, 'Two Days with God and the General'!

Peter: I remember reading one of Campbell Morgan's books a number of years ago.

Sally: I wonder if it was the same book of which a retired officer speaks. A long time ago, he was preparing a Bible message based on the Lord's prayer - 'Forgive us our debts ...' He discovered that the Latin word for debt is *debeo,* 'I owe'. He also discovered that *debeo* has the parallel meaning 'I ought'. Trigger! 'Our oughts are our debts'. A message outline quickly came together. 'Forgive us our debts .... our debts are our 'oughts'. When we ought to do this or that, we are in debt to ourselves to do it, we are in debt to our fellow, and we are in debt to God'. That message outline proved a good servant to the officer for many a year. Then one day he came across exactly that sermon structure in Campbell Morgan's book. From that point on he never used the message again lest some well-read comrade in the congregation should charge him, 'Ah, I know where you got that one from!'

Now, we must be on our way home, Peter.

On Location
at THQ
'The Bible Says . . .'

THE 53 Bus from Blackheath brought Major Sally and Peter to the Elephant and Castle, the name of an old public house, incorporated long since into a large, pink shopping/office complex, but still a well-known London traffic nexus.

The new THQ could hardly be more conveniently placed, Salvationist Publishing and Supplies Ltd riding pillion behind the nine-floor tower block. They arrived just in time to 'corner' Colonel Gordon Becker, one of the Army's finest finance minds, who was leaving within a matter of hours for auditing duties at Salvation Army headquarters in Indonesia.

During General Paul Rader's term of office, the then Territorial Commander, Commr Dinsdale Pender conveyed a surprising and unexpected message to his Cabinet — that IHQ wanted to redevelop 101 Queen Victoria Street, so could the Territory seek alternative accommodation! Without doubt a difficult task, especially with the financial constraints necessary following the fraud perpetrated on them some years previously.

So the search began. Property consultants were engaged to carry out a search for buildings which might be suitable for a new Territorial Headquarters. Several visits each month over many months became the norm, when the TC, accompanied by Colonels Davis, Logan and Becker travelled throughout London and suburbia in search of the ideal premises.

Some thirty or more premises were inspected, including a huge building in Kings Cross with an underground car park for 100 cars, a beautiful listed building in the heart of the city, complete with ornate entrance and large chandeliers, a new tower block in Docklands with exterior cladding in blue glass (ideal, but what would the public think?). Ultimately the ideal proved to be close at hand and very central.

A large glass-fronted building in Elephant and Castle had recently been vacated by one of the many Government quangos of the time. It was available if we moved quickly. What we found was not quite what we expected, a concrete shell with huge circular pillars on each floor and numerous concrete holes drilled apparently in haphazard fashion throughout. Surely this could not be it, but the THQ Property team led by Mr Alan Vince felt differently and with visionary planning they convinced us that it was. And so it proved to be.

Many months of prayer, meticulous attention to detail and not a little soul-searching followed and in due time the vision, managed entirely by our own THQ property staff, became reality. The building which cost in excess of £5 million with a similar amount spent on refurbishment, opened in the early days of 1999 and was debt free. How did that happen?

Well, the sale of the long leasehold recently renewed with the Duke of Westminster on the old Judd Street premises realised a considerable sum when purchased by the Royal National Institute for the Blind. Also there was in existence a carefully guarded letter signed by General Eva Burrows and written at the time of the separation of the Territory from IHQ, acknowledging that as and when it became necessary, the Territory had an 'equity interest' in the Queen Victoria Street site. The 'as and when' became now, and true to its word, IHQ over time made good its promise to the Territory in financial terms. Along with central funding set aside for such an eventuality, this enabled the total cost of both purchase and refurbishment to be met.

The Territory moved into its modern and functional premises – from 101 to 101 (from Queen Victoria Street to Newington Causeway), debt free.

Gordon Becker, Colonel

Aftersight and Foresight (4)

We believe that the Scriptures of the Old and New Testaments were given by inspiration of God and that they only constitute the Divine rule of Christian faith and practice.

Doctrine 1

Sally: Here we are in the foyer of Territorial Headquarters, control centre of the Army in the UK and the Republic of Ireland. Did you enjoy your visit to IHQ?

Peter: Fascinating. What a mighty oak tree has grown from an East London acorn. I had almost forgotten.

Sally: It is the Lord's doing and it is marvellous in our eyes. Did the chat about our second Doctrine help?

Peter: I'm afraid that the most I can manage at the moment is, 'I believe in God, the source of all life, to whom all life returns'

Sally: I don't analyse like you, Peter. I enjoy my work, I love my people.

Peter: When you gave me a copy of the articles of war to read you did say that I could ask questions on any point, didn't you?

Sally: You have other questions?

Peter: Yes, about Doctrine 1.

Sally: We believe that the Scriptures of the Old and New Testament were given by inspiration of God and that they only constitute the Divine rule of Christian faith and practice.

Peter: For starters – Christian Practice?

Sally: That means Christian service, or living.

Peter: Then why not say so? Ideas command, words can confuse.

By the way, do you know how 'Elephant and Castle' got its name? Edward I of England travelled to Spain in 1254 to marry Princess Eleanor. He was 15, she was 9. Eleanor's title was 'La Infanta De Castile'. The local Londoners soon changed that into 'Elephant and Castle' — language update.

Sally: Now a bustling hub of South London traffic and not an elephant in sight.

Peter: May I ask about that first Doctrine, about the Bible being inspired by God?

Sally: The Bible is a very special book. I read from it every night before dropping off to sleep.

Peter: Much of the Bible is certainly inspiring, but does the first Doctrine claim too much?

Sally: Prime Minister Gladstone called the Bible 'The Impregnable Rock of Holy Scripture'

Peter: Is the Bible impregnable?

Much of the text is certainly inspiring but not all of it surely? For the past three Sunday mornings you have led us on a Cook's tour round and round a place called Jericho.

Sally: My message was intended to encourage you all to face up to difficulties in your Christian service and to over-come them.

Peter: But why go back thousands of years into Hebrew pre-history, perhaps mythology, to a story of carnage and genocide, to tell us that?

Sally: At a time of deep personal need, Major Yvonne Field found peace of heart in reading Exodus 33:13-16. She made the prayer recorded there her own and penned, 'If Your Presence'.

IF YOUR PRESENCE

Lord, if your presence does not go with us,
Please do not send us up from here.
How will anyone know we are your people
Unless you go before us?

Lord if your favour does not rest on us,
We dare not move beyond this place.
How will anyone know we go in your name
Unless your blessing is over us?

So we stand within your presence
And humbly seek your grace;
Father, Almighty, Jehovah, Saviour,
We long to meet you face to face.
Let your glory fall upon us;
Convict, inspire, provide.
Father, Almighty, Jehovah, Saviour,
Your holy presence is our guide.

Lord, if your presence does not stay with us,
Please do not send us up from here.
How will anyone hear of truth and goodness
Unless your Word speaks through us?
Lord, if your presence is not love in us,
How can we minister your grace?
How will anyone feel your tender mercy
Unless your heart is in us?

Peter: Those lines come from the heart and they reach mine.

Sally: A piece of Hebrew history recorded by a Hebrew historian and transformed into a deeply moving Christian meditation.

Peter: But I have to say that by and large I find the Old

Testament to be little more than the history of an ancient Hebrew tribe, recorded by Hebrew historians. And all historians view the story of their nation through rose-tinted spectacles, you know.

Sally: The Old Testament is part of the Bible, and I accept it as such.

Peter: Shall I tell you what I think Major?

Long before the dawn of history a migrating tribe of Bedouin wandered into the fertile plain between the Euphrates and the Nile. For the first time they could sow crops and reap harvests. It dawned on some good men and true of the tribe that they should give thanks for their new way of life. They named one God Jehovah, and began to worship him. Then they made Jehovah their tribal deity. He would fight their battles for them. All other tribes were anathema to him. When you talk to us about Joshua and Jericho, I hear a Jewish historian speaking.

Sally: I think you are playing games, our doctrine does not claim literal, verbal inspiration. We could do with a few statesmen like the prophet Amos today. 'Let judgement run down as waters and righteousness as a mighty stream'[1].

Peter: I agree. Politicians look to the next election, statesmen look to the next generation. But, you know, even the prophets were historians in their own way. They called the nation back to an ideal past, the good old days.

Sally: I haven't the time or inclination to analyse like you, Peter. For me the Bible is the inspired word of God. It would be easier to empty the Mediterranean with a teaspoon than exhaust the Bible of its meaning and truth. God the creator is found in the Old Testament. Jesus Christ of Nazareth steps out of the pages of the New Testament.

---

[1] Amos 5:24

Peter: So much of the Bible is inspiring, but if we simply say 'the Bible says ...' and leave it at that, we have problems.

Much of the Old Testament seems to be written in the style of Roald Dahl. Scare the kids to death, they love it! Open the Old Testament at almost any page and you hear the scratch of the pens of Hebrew historians.

This is true not only when we read of bloody conquest and victory over rival tribes. Beyond the recorded words of lyricist or prophet, or philosopher or poet, all its history is 'patriotic' history. Hebrew historians no less than other historians favour their nation. Having made Jehovah their tribal deity, Hebrew historians had no hesitation in claiming him as their commander in battle.

Even the prophets seem to do so.

Sally: Stop knocking, Peter.

Peter: I'm not knocking the Bible, Major. I reverence it highly but I *am* asking 'Is the whole Bible inspired by God?'

The letters to churches in the New Testament would repay a lifetime's reflection (although you for one would surely query St Paul's apparent anti-feminism).

Sally: The four gospels record the inspiring story of the life and teaching of Jesus Christ.

Peter: Keep on telling us the story, Major. I remember singing as a child:

> Tell me the story of Jesus,
> Write on my heart every word. [2]

But is everything in the New Testament inspired? Did Jesus Christ really become an after-dinner conjurer at a village wedding? [3] Shall I tell you what I think possibly happened?

---

[2] *SASB* 99
[3] John 2:1ff

Jesus went into the kitchen to thank the ladies for an excellent meal, like you did on Christmas Day. He asked, 'Can I do anything to help?' Perhaps he moved an empty water jar or two from here to there, when, surprise, surprise, revealed for all to see, there stood a wine jar, filled to the brim, overlooked in the excitement and busyness of the day.

Legends grow around commanding personalities, you know. And to insist on a sleight of hand with wine bottles is to diminish Jesus of Nazareth, the Prince of Glory, to a kind of 'Dr Who'.

Sally: I shall not hesitate to read the village wedding story at the next Army wedding I conduct.

Peter: Then I hope you will tell the story as a three-dimensional parable. Tell the happy couple that the honeymoon cannot last forever. Life will not always sparkle like wine. Familiarity, anxiety about health, financial pressures and other problems may sour the bubbling wine of marriage until it tastes like tepid water. Tolerance, the will to make a go of it and mutual respect could recover the sparkle.

Sally: There is so much in the Bible that is inspiring.

Peter: And it is not difficult to see how the word inspiring has changed into 'inspired'. Think of the record of Christ's Transfiguration. The simplest explanation of any profundity is likely to be the correct explanation.

Transfiguration means 'seeing a person or situation in a new light.' Chatter about Christ's clothing being 'whiter than white' with side references to 'Persil' or 'Daz' are unworthy of the preacher and belittling to the congregation. I have been re-reading the Bible story following Colonel Margaret Hay's contribution to *Salvationist* last July.

Sally: So have I. Here are three 'Reflections'.

Reflections from the Mount of Transfiguration
(Luke 9:18-42)

'Transfiguration' - seeing a person or situation
with clearer discernment.

Reflection I

*At Caesarea Philippi, confirmed on the Mount of Transfiguration,
Jesus sees himself more clearly than at any previous time.*

1. The 40 days, 40 nights of Christ's wilderness temptations
   are best understood as prolonged self-questioning. 'Who
   am I?' 'How do I achieve my goal?' Do I go for ...
   a. Imperial power?   (all the kingdoms of the world...)
   b. Ecclesiastical power? (pinnacle of the temple....)
   c. Industrial power?   (stones into bread...)'

2. Unfinished business! 'The devil left him for a while'.[4]

3. Actions speak louder than words. 'Go and do something,'
   our Founder charged Bramwell. Positive action can help
   straighten out tentative reflection. Refusing to wait for the
   mists of uncertainty to clear, Jesus:
   a. Visits Nazareth and announces his manifesto.[5]
   b. Begins his healing ministry 'At even, e'er the sun
      was set...'[6]
   c. Sets up his support group.[7]

4. But busy days are not the complete answer for a restless
   mind or troubled spirit.

   At Caesarea Philippi the uncertainty hauntingly returns:
   'Who am I?', articulated as a question to the disciples,
   'Who do *you* say that I am?' Jesus finds the answer to his
   soul-search in Peter's recognition: — 'You are the Messiah
   of God'[8].

---

[4] Luke 4:13
[5] Luke 4:16-28
[6] Luke 4:40,41 also *SASB* 558
[7] Mark 1:16-20, Luke 5:10-11, John 1:35-46 record it in different ways
[8] Luke 9:18-20

5. Peace of mind at last — at least, until Gethsemane.
    Under the shadow of the Roman fortress of Caesarea
    Philippi, perhaps even at that moment within sound of
    the tramping feet of a passing military platoon, Jesus
    recognises this answer to his self-questioning. He spells
    out, for himself primarily, the implications of His
    Nazareth manifesto:

> The Son of man must suffer much and be rejected by the elders,
> the chief priests and the teachers of the law. He will be put to
> death ... If anyone wants to come with me, he must forget self,
> take up his cross every day and follow me... [9]

6. The mists lift for our Lord. He now sees himself and his
    mission clearly, as we, by grace, have come to see him, and
    our own life's purpose, clearly. Symbolically he leads Peter,
    James and John, to the top of a hill, and I am reminded of
    the following verses by Harry Kemp:

> I saw the conquerors riding by
>   With cruel lips and faces wan;
> Musing on kingdoms sacked and burned,
>   There rode the Mongol, Genghis Khan;
>
> And Alexander, like a god,
>   Who sought to weld the world in one;
> And Caesar with his laurel wreath;
>   And like a thing from hell, the Hun.
>
> And, leading like a star, the van
>   Heedless of upstretched arm and groan,
> Inscrutable Napoleon went,
>   Dreaming of Empire and alone . . .
>
> Then all they perished from the earth
>   As fleeting shadows from a glass;
> And, conquering down the centuries,
>   Came Christ, the Swordless, on an ass.

---

[9] Luke 9:22,23

Reflection II

*Peter, James and John see Jesus more clearly than
at any time previously.*

1. You only have one chance to make a first impression.[10]
   The synoptic gospels record the first impression made by
   Jesus on those early disciples.[11]

   > By the peaceful shores of Galilee
   > Mending their nets by the silvery sea,
   > The fishermen toiled at the their task each day
   > Till the Master walketh along that way.[12]

2. John's gospel gives an alternative account — not Galilee,
   but on Jordan's banks. It wasn't Simon Peter who first
   recognised the Messiah, but Andrew his brother, says the
   Johannine version.[13]

   > Convinced and constrained by just a few hours in Christ's
   > company, conversation continuing far into the night, Andrew
   > sought out Simon his brother and burst out, 'We have found
   > the Messiah!' Some days later, now by the shore of Galilee, the
   > introduction became an invitation, 'Jesus saw Simon and
   > Andrew his brother casting a net into the sea ... and said,
   > 'Come after me and I will make you fishers of men.[14]

3. But at Caesarea Philippi uncertainty lingers.
   'Who am I?' asked Jesus.
   'Some say this, some say that,' they answered.
   Not Peter.
   'You are the Messiah of God!' he exploded.
   And it seems reasonable to suppose that, trudging up
   the 9,000 feet of Mount Hermon, John and James
   'quizzed' Peter about what he had said. They began to see
   Jesus in a clearer light and to see themselves as more than
   mere followers of a new Rabbi.

---

[10] Public Relations mantra
[11] Matthew 4:18-22
[12] *SASB* 680
[13] John 1:35-42
[14] *Christus Victor* p.554, based on Mark 1:16ff

> Lead me higher up the mountain
> Give me fellowship with thee,
> In thy light I see the fountain
> And the blood now cleanses me.[15]

4. Jesus was transfigured, they themselves were transfigured. Even time was transfigured for them.

They remembered their nation's historic past: dreamed of two patriarchs, Moses and Elijah. And they wanted this present, transforming hour to continue into the future and for ever. Three tents would help — to mark the occasion in a traditional Hebrew manner, but this was not a time to stand still and contemplate, even though their Master was the Lord of time.

> Time is too slow for those who wait,
> Too swift for those who fear,
> Too long for those who grieve,
> Too short for those who rejoice,
> But for those who love time is eternal.[16]

5. We too may look back to the hour and place of our own transformed view of ourselves. the point at which Christ was to be all in all, and we would be his for ever.

Dr W. R. Matthews, who was Dean of St.Paul's Cathedral 1934-67, writes of his personal transfiguration as a youthful bank clerk in the City:

> I now come to an incident which I regard as a kind of divine guidance, and which changed the course of my existence... The experience stands out from the normal and common-place as though it had a timeless existence...It was a summer day when the sun flooded even Bishopsgate with glory.
>
> I had been in the London office of the Swiss Banking Corporation on some routine business, and as I came down the steps into the full light of the sun, I suddenly felt that the sun was in me...I was taken hold of by a power or a Spirit, which filled me with joy and peace and courage. My doubts

---

[15] *SASB* 429
[16] Henry van Dyke (1852-1933)

about God were transcended. He needed me and called me...
Exultant happiness carried me away. I knew and felt that God
was real and that I was a child of God.

It seems to me that from that moment I knew I should be
refusing some kind of a divine call if l did not break away from
the routine in which I was becoming settled. I did not take this
as a definite call to priesthood, or to any office in the Church,
but as a summons to make a choice....[17]

> Don't stay in the valley,
>   Where the shadows fall;
> Climb up to the mountain top,
>   'Tis the sweetest place of all;
> Catch the heavenly breezes,
>   Live in God's sunshine;
> Doubts and fears will flee away,
>   You'll be happy all the time.[18]

Reflection III

*At the foot of the mountain a distraught father sees
Jesus to be more than a teacher.*

1. 'A man shouted from the crowd, Teacher! I beg you, look
   on my son - my only son!'[19] The boy, an epileptic from
   birth, is calmed. His father bows low in the presence of
   Jesus the healer. The crowd cheers as the father embraces
   his restored son.

> The great physician now is near,
>   The sympathising Jesus;
> He speaks, the drooping heart to cheer;
>   O hear the voice of Jesus! [20]

2. That Jesus himself perceived the connection between his
   healing ministry and his redemptive mission is obvious
   from such a saying as, 'They that are whole have no need

---

[17] *Memories and Meanings* p.47
[18] *SASB* Chorus 116
[19] Luke 9:38
[20] *SASB* 67

of a physician, but they that are sick: I came not to call the righteous but sinners' (Mark 2:17).[21] A Christian doctor is possibly closer to the mind of Christ than the rest of us can hope to be. And even a doctor without faith is not far from the Lord, even if he is not so aware. Let us each hold our own GP in ever-increasing appreciation as he/she toils on the front line of the battle against disease, disorder and decay. My own GP, Dr. Martin Powell, cares for 2,300 patients, God sustain him.

3. The Church celebrates the Transfiguration of Christ each year on 6 August.

In *Salvationist,* 6 August 2005, Colonel Margaret Hay pointed out the irony of another transfiguring brightness — the dropping of the atomic bomb on Hiroshima sixty years earlier, 6 August 1945. A horror repeated three days later on Nagasaki, 9 August 1945. Margaret writes of a Japanese doctor, Dr Takashi Nagai:

> When the bomb fell on Nagasaki, Dr Nagai worked to the limit of his strength with patients evacuated to the summit of a nearby hill. Nagai, a Christian, was more than a doctor, he was an apostle of charity. He wrote: 'The doctor's job is to suffer and rejoice with his patients, to learn to diminish their suffering as if it were his own.' Nagai made the most stricken area of Nagasaki his 'home'. He constructed a makeshift dwelling — a few metal sheets resting against a wall. Nagai was dying. He had been given the last rites. Lying on his back, writing on a small chalkboard, he wrote: 'What shall we do with this double-edged sword hidden in the universe by God and now discovered by man? ... The decision rests in the freewill of man ... I believe that a true religious spirit is the sole guarantee in this area' ... The Transfiguration of Christ and the events of August 1945 are seen to intersect. As we read the gospels through the lens of history, we see more clearly the transfigured Lord, the hope of the nations, and hear again, 'This is my Son, whom I love. Listen to him.'

---

[21] Alan Richardson, *A Theological Word Book of the Bible* p.103

O touch me again, Lord,
Touch me again,
This moment I feel
Afresh thou canst heal!
So touch me again, Lord,
O touch me again! [22]

Peter: And the book of Revelation? There's no-man's land for you, a field strewn with anti-personnel mines.

I remember a sermon from years ago. The officer took half a text from the book of Revelation, added to it half a text from the book of Daniel and, as I recall, we finished up with the Pope's telephone number! The Book of Revelation is a tract for hard times, a coded message to encourage persecuted Christians fighting for their very lives.

Dr Burnett wrote:

> The Book of Revelation was written for no other purpose than to brace and hearten God's people, the Christian Church, around the year 95 of our era, when the Emperor Domitian began his great persecutions. Domitian decreed that every Christian had to declare himself. The crisis was grave and acute. No physical resistance could be offered by the Christian – none that would not be ridiculous. Nor was any escape possible, for whither throughout the length and breadth of the Roman Empire could one flee from Caesar? Secrecy was also out of the question. To be not a very zealous Christian was not enough for safety: to be safe one must be an avowed pagan. Steps were taken to see that the challenge to declare oneself faced every human being in the province (of Asia). The pagan multitude, who regarded the Christian position with incredulity and hatred, and the local priesthood in whose interest it was to further the worship of the State, saw to it that every one suspected of Christian sympathies either paid homage to the Emperor Domitian, or paid the penalty. [23]

---

[22] *SASB* Chorus 92
[23] *The Lord Reigneth* p.43

That makes more sense than dissertations about the mark of the beast, or 666, or whether Napoleon or Hitler or Stalin was anti-Christ. May I ask you another question?

Sally: About our first doctrine? Go ahead

Peter: Can I ask about this word 'only'? The Scriptures are the *only* guide to Christian faith and practice?

Sally: Salvationist Bill Metcalf writes:

> Perhaps it would be more precise and therefore more helpful to say that the Scriptures constitute the ultimate written source of Christian faith and practice. It would still distinguish them from all other writings which have been put forward through the centuries as definitive truth.

Peter: Such as?

Sally: The writings of other faiths, the rules of monastic orders, liturgies, and so on.

Peter: Salvation Army *Orders and Regulations*?

Sally: Now, now!

Peter: You speak of the Bible as 'the word of God'.

Sally: The phrase 'the word of God' has at least three meanings.

1. The word of God is a written word contained in a book – the Bible;
2. Jesus Christ is the incarnate Word: 'The word became flesh and dwelt among us —

Peter: [interrupts]— and we beheld His glory, the glory as of the only begotten of the Father, full of grace and truth.'[24] There's inspiration for you!

Sally: 3. And the word of God also comes as guidance from the Holy Spirit, as it did to John the Baptist in the wilderness[25] and, of course, to Jesus himself.

Peter: The answer my friend is blowing in the wind. Something like that — the breath of the Holy Spirit.

---

[24] John 1:14 *KJV*
[25] Luke 3:2

Sally: Acts 6 describes the growth of the early Church in this way: 'The word of God increased' — a further pointer to 'the word of God' meaning more than printed words on the page of a book; but the Bible is also rightly referred to as the word of God.

> Holy Bible, book divine,
> Precious treasure, thou art mine.[26]

I believe the Bible to be inspired by God.

Peter: I believe that the Scriptures of the Old Testament reveal the aspirations after God of many people through many generations and the inspiration which came to them.

I believe that the Scriptures of the New Testament tell the story of the life and teaching of Jesus Christ and the inspiration which came to many people as they thought and talked and wrote about Him.

God needs no championing. Why is it that Christian writers and preachers sometimes find it so difficult to acknowledge the contradictions in the Bible?

It would help people like me if they were prepared to do so. Did the Reformation replace an infallible Pope with an infallible book? I get the impression sometimes that I am being urged to stop thinking, and to 'just believe', like the schoolboy who defined faith as 'believing what you know ain't true'.

There is absolutely no way of explaining natural disasters, or to account for a child born with spina bifida, but God is innocent of all charges, case dismissed.

Sally: It's the Fall, Peter, the Devil at work.

Peter: Sorry, Major, I dismiss that charge, too. It would be to award to his satanic majesty powers he does not possess.

Sally: The man of no faith says 'I don't understand, so I can't believe.'

---

[26] *SASB* 652

Peter: 'Faith is the substance of things hoped for, the evidence of things not seen'.[26] The good Lord seems to have prescribed dark glasses for us all for the time being. Twenty-twenty vision is promised in the future, I believe.

Sally: No pilgrims journey to Plumstead cemetery in south east London to keep vigil at the grave of a poet of whom the world will never learn. He rests for ever under the shadow of his belovèd Bostall Woods. He penned his own farewell. His words can be read on the simple headstone.

DAWN

This is the dawning of the day,
The promised May of winter's hopes,
The time when Spring begins again,
When newness springs itself without refrain,
When life creates itself in love, and, without shame,
Without a backward glance at winter's bane,
Without a vengeful glance for the corruptive pain
That brings the cold and dark; when those that have,
Treat those that don't with arrogant disdain.
No! Spring does every year forgive what winter did
And so, released from hate,
Shines out the light in winter hid.

(Paul Hunter, 1946-2000)

Peter: Resurrection!

Sally: Here's a copy of *Words of Life* the Army's Bible reading aid, published in conjunction with Hodder and Stoughton. Try to find time to read it.

Peter: Seated in the foyer of THQ one meets the world and his wife. Who are these friends coming towards us?

Sally: Our Territorial Leaders, Commissioners John and Elizabeth Matear. 'Commissioner, may I introduce Peter to you? He is going to be one of your soldiers.'

---

[26] Hebrews 11:1

On Location
at Sunbury Court
'Totally depraved' — Who? Me?

TWO OR THREE weeks later, Major Sally called for Peter at his home. The journey across London from east to west, and on out to Sunbury-on-Thames, Surrey, would be hardly more than 20 miles, but it took them all of 95 minutes.

In anticipation Major Storey had touched base with the Army's International Heritage Centre, Denmark Hill. What could they tell her about the history of Sunbury Court? Director Major Stephen Grinsted referred the enquiry to Beccy Hine, research assistant, who did her her homework thoroughly.

> Sunbury Court is situated in the village of Sunbury-on-Thames and stands in 22 acres of private land. Edward the Confessor 'confirmed the Manor unto the Abbot of Westminster', and in the sixteenth century the manor formed part of a grant under the Great Seal of England to Sir Robert Killigrew of the Manor of Colkemington(Kempton). During the reigns of the Plantagenet Kings(1154-1399), the manor was used as a royal palace, with the building — then known as Sunbury House — possibly being used as an annex to the palace.

Although structurally the building has changed very little, Sunbury Court saw a number of owners before The Salvation Army took possession in 1925.

The Court's last private owner was William Horatio Harfield who rebuilt the present east and west wings after a fire during his residency. After his death the property became the Sunbury Court Club but the building was empty in 1925 when General Bramwell Booth and his son Wycliffe, who was also his ADC, saw Sunbury Court's potential as a suitable building for the International Training Institute, to give officers throughout the world further training.

After some reconstruction Sunbury Court made an ideal conference centre, for example; transforming the panelled hall into a lecture room complete with platform and Army flag; the library into a prayer room and the drawing room with its original painted murals by the Swedish painter and engraver, Elias Martin, into the dining room.

After being used as a conference centre for several years, Sunbury Court served as an Eventide Home until General Evangeline Booth decided that it should again be used for conferences but with the emphasis being on youth.

This led to the addition of a swimming pool, a boating pond, playgrounds and a camping site. There was also an open-air 'Temple of Youth' constructed, where camp-fire meetings could be held.

As the Second World War began the youth centre closed and Sunbury Court was used by officers, soldiers and friends in order to relax and escape the hazards of war. Some stayed long-term and others came for holiday weeks.

After the War, Sunbury Court was used as a conference centre once more and of course has been used to host all but two High Councils. (In 1934 and 1939 the High Council met at Clapton).

There have been several additions made to the facilities at Sunbury Court, including a new recreational centre in 1980 and the newest being the International Conference Centre opened by General Paul Rader in 1999.

Beccy Hine,
International Heritage Centre

Aftersight and Foresight (5)

… All men have become totally depraved … justly exposed to the wrath of God … we believe in … the endless punishment of the wicked.

Doctrines 5 & 11

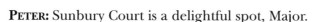

PETER: Sunbury Court is a delightful spot, Major.

Sally: A Thameside jewel, well kept grounds, the walls of the Court saturated with the prayers and praise of many generations, including all but two of our High Councils.

Peter: Hardly the place at which to ask you about 'The endless punishment of the wicked'.

Sally: Is that what you want to talk about, our eleventh Doctrine? I'll listen, remembering that Romans 14:1 says, 'Receive him that is weak in the faith … but not to doubtful disputations'.

Peter: Doubtful disputations?

Sally: Roughly translated – Nitpicking!

Peter: Is that what I seem to be doing? I am asking serious questions about serious matters of serious concern to me. You did say I could ask questions.

Sally: I begin to see where you are coming from Peter, but, as I say, I am too busy, too happily busy to analyse like you wish to do.

Peter: Why do so many Christians cling so tenaciously to the idea of hell-fire? A journalist reporting an evangelical campaign wrote: 'He (the evangelist) spoke passionately of Hell but there were no tears in his eyes'.

Sally: God is righteous. To reject wrong-doing is of his very nature, his DNA.

Peter: A Bedouin tribe migrates from the deserts of Arabia, into the fertile plain between the Euphrates and the Nile. They are able now to plant crops and reap harvests. They awake to the truth that there can only be one God, 'Jehovah', and begin to worship him.

In time they adopt him as their tribal deity. He belongs to them and to no other tribe. They believe he will go into battle with them. All other tribes are anathema to their God. The tribal deity of those early Bedouin has become the judging God of Christian misunderstanding. Westminster Abbey has transmuted into the Old Bailey.

Sally: Micah the prophet declared 'Woe to them that devise iniquity and work evil on their beds...' [1]

Peter: I read that he also wrote, 'Who is a God like unto thee that pardoneth iniquity and doth not retain his anger for ever because he delights in mercy?' [2]

Sally: Shall not the judge of all the earth do right? [3]

Peter: But to say so in outmoded language is a calumny against him. Jesus said, 'When you pray, say, Our Father...'

Sally: All wrongdoing bears within itself the seeds of its own decay.

Peter: That is absolutely right. Sow wild oats, eat bitter porridge.

Sally: And wrong-doing must be punished.

Peter: Society sees to that with punishment that fits the crime and the Criminal Records Bureau takes note. Justice is done and is seen to be done. But does God keep records like that? Does he have closed-circuit television? Has he a microfilm record of your life and mine?

Sally: Not only does society pass judgement, our conscience is a personal magistrate.

[1] Micah 2:1
[2] Micah 7:18
[3] Genesis 18:25

Peter: That I can believe. The molecules of my brain have registered my sins against me.

Sally: There is a magistrate's court within every one of us. We are each our own prosecuting counsel.

The prodigal son asked his father for punishment, not forgiveness. He passed judgement on himself.

Peter: He said to his Father 'I have sinned… I am no longer worthy of being your son, make me a servant in your household' [4]

Sally: And the Father threw a banquet for him.

Peter: Preachers talk about the prodigal son. They should talk more about the prodigal Father. Prodigal means 'lavish'. God surely is lavish in mercy. Believing this I have found the things which belong to my peace.

Sally: But the boy did repent. He did return home, you know.

Peter: His father went looking for him long before his son took the first step.

Sally: 'Then how much more shall God our Father in love forgive…' [5] But some people seem to have no conscience.

Peter: They live in a hell of their own creation, total moral desuetude, with no signposts pointing the way out to confession, forgiveness, light and freedom.

Sally: In our hostels the officer will tell the men, 'God will forgive your transgressions and remember them no more'[6] but many do not hear. They cannot forgive themselves. They have lost so much.

Peter: We are all fragile people. God knows our frame, he remembers that we are dust.

Sally: St. Paul teaches that we shall all appear before the judgement seat of Christ.[7]

---

[4] Luke 15:19
[5] *SASB* 50
[6] *SASB* 272
[7] 2 Corinthians 5:10

Peter: On the road to Damascus Saul accepted Christ's mercy.
Between the saddle and the ground
I mercy sought and mercy found!'[8]

Sally: But some people can only be described as wicked. Just think of the Soham murders.

Peter: Society has pronounced judgement. May God have mercy on that man's soul. Have you heard of the Rembrandt Research Project? Rembrandt painted many self-portraits, all immediately identifiable by his round chin and gentle eyes. A pupil of Rembrandt's painted over one of his master's self-portraits.

Sally: Why would he do that?

Peter: Maybe for practice, perhaps he could not afford to buy canvas for himself.

Sally: What did he paint?

Peter: A Russian nobleman. A research project was launched a few years ago. The superimposed painting was removed by scalpel, layer after layer. It took six years of painstaking labour. The original Rembrandt now hangs in Rembrandt's house in Amsterdam, estimated value, $30,000,000.

Sally: Genuine?

Peter: Identified by the round chin and the gentle eyes.

Sally: 'Behind a frowning providence he hides a smiling face'.[9]

Peter: Like the judgement seat of Christ.

Sally: You said that Saul stood before Christ on the Damascus road. The prophet Isaiah wrote about the suffering servant and the judgement he pronounces. Isaiah saw his own Hebrew nation as God's suffering servant. For us the suffering servant is Jesus Christ.

---

[8] Acts 9:4 Quote adapted from Katharine Tynan's poem 'The Great Mercy'
[9] *SASB* 29

Peter: The man for others like no man before him nor any man since.

Sally: Isaiah wrote:

> Here is my servant whom I have chosen, the one I love and with whom I am pleased. I will send my spirit upon him and he will announce my judgement to the nations. He will not argue or shout or make loud speeches in the streets. He will be gentle to those who are weak and kind to those who are helpless. He will persist until he causes justice to triumph and on him will all peoples put their hope.[10]

Peter: A smoking flax he will not quench.[10]

Sally: A bruised reed he will not break.[10]

Peter: The book of Exodus tells of the destruction (by God) of an Egyptian army in the Red Sea.

> And Miriam ... took a timbrel in her hand; and all the women went out after her with timbrels and with dances. And Miriam answered them, "Sing ye to the Lord for he hath triumphed gloriously. The horse and his rider hath he thrown into the sea".[11]

I've no idea who Rabbi Johanan was, or where and when he lived. But a Jew of our own age, Victor Gollancz, quotes him in his book *A Year of Grace*, which was published during World War II as an appeal for love to triumph over hatred:

> The ministering angels wanted to sing a hymn at the destruction of the Egyptians, but God said, 'My children lie drowned in the sea, and you would sing?'

Sally: Rabbi Johanan possessed the spirit of Christ.

Peter: A man for others, a voice crying in the wilderness. Will you help me to understand the other words in the eleventh Doctrine?

Sally: Not now. Let's go for a walk by the riverside and look at the swans. They also have found the things which belong to their peace.

---

[10] Isaiah 42:1ff
[11] Exodus 15:20,21

On Location
in Croydon Centre
Life beyond Life

CROYDON is a thriving, bustling south London borough. It was massively re-developed at the end of World War II with Manhattan-style high-rise blocks. Day-time car-parking mid-week in the courtyard at the front of the citadel presents little problem. But come early at weekends!

Remembering that veteran Colonel Brindley Boon is a soldier of the Croydon Citadel corps, Major Sally telephoned him. Had he a Croydon story he could share with her?

Croydon Citadel Corps has enjoyed happy ecumenical relationships with the neighbouring parish church of St. John's for many years. In 1968 Major Leslie Condon took the Croydon Citadel Band, of which he was bandmaster, to St. John's for a commemoration festival. Colonel Brindley Boon accompanied the band. Brindley was so overwhelmed by the beauty of the service that he was moved to write what is now song 528 in the Salvation Army Song Book:

> Thou art holy, Lord of glory
>> From thy altar blessings flow;
> I, unworthy, kneel before thee,
>> Cleanse from sin and peace bestow.

Major Leslie Condon was promoted to Glory while leading the Citadel Band in Croydon High Street on Christmas Eve, 1983. Leslie's funeral service was held in the Croydon Citadel hall on New Year's Day, 1984.

Two bands participated in the service; the International Staff Band, (of which Leslie was deputy bandmaster) and Croydon Citadel Band.

At the conclusion of the service the two bands formed a corridor of honour in the courtyard at the front of the Citadel. An eerie silence fell upon the sorrowing crowd as Leslie was borne along this avenue of grieving musicians.

Above the noise of London's traffic, we heard the tolling of the Passing Bell.

St. John's was mourning too.

Aftersight and Foresight (6)

'We believe in the immortality of the soul, in the resurrection of the body …

Doctrine 11

PETER: What a delightful place – spacious, airy, large windows. Let me see, 25, 30 tables – there are probably forty other people enjoying the facilities with us.

Sally: Good food, at hardly-more-than-cost prices, and service with a smile.

Peter: Are all these people sitting here Salvationists?

Sally: This community centre is available to all-comers, an asset to the neighbourhood.

Peter: A bang-up-to-date facility.

Sally: The Croydon Citadel corps, of which this community centre is an essential part, was the 9th Christian Mission centre opened in Booth's time. It is now the second oldest corps – Poplar is the oldest.

Peter: An historic corps meeting the contemporary situation. Where does that door over there lead?

Sally: Direct communication with the meeting hall. When you have finished your dessert, I'll take you through.

Peter: Good congregations?

Sally: Of all ages, including scores of delightful young people.

Peter: Music?

Sally: Superb, first class band – as a former bandsman you would appreciate the band – an equally pleasing songster brigade, and the youth music groups are a joy to eye and ear. By the way, you must look in at the adjoining Lighthouse youth centre before you leave, another state-of-the-art facility. But tell me, what is it you want to talk about today?

Peter: I have a soul, haven't I? I have believed it all my life.

Sally: They said you were the life and soul of the party at our corps New Year's Eve dinner, Peter.

Peter: And not a glass of wine in sight!

Sally: Your soul is not something you add on, an attachment of some sort. Soul is you, the real you. 'The Lord God formed man of the dust of the ground and breathed into his nostrils the breath of life and man became a living soul.' [1]

Peter: And we Salvationists believe in the immortality of the soul – it never dies?

Sally: John Coutts has written:

> Made in the image of God, each child has been endowed with a soul as well as a mind and a body. The soul in relationship with its creator can survive the physical dissolution of the brain (as following a stroke) ... Both the soul and the mind make up the self which operates through the brain. [2]

Peter: This night I lay me down to sleep,
I pray thee, God, my soul to keep;

---

[1] Genesis 2:7

[2] *Salvationist* 7 January 2006

> And if I die before I wake,
> I pray thee, God, my soul to take.

Sally: A very special prayer, Peter.

Peter: Did Jesus Christ have anything to say about 'soul'?

Sally: 'What shall it profit a man if he shall gain the whole world and lose his own soul?' [3]

Peter: I remember. 'Or what shall a man give in exchange for his soul?'[3]

Sally: Jesus also told us to 'Love the Lord your God with all your heart, and with all your soul, and with all your mind, and with all your strength' [4]

Peter: 'And your neighbour as yourself' ... the son of man, the man for others, like no man before him nor any man since.

Sally: The face is the image of the soul.

Peter: Why do so many people wear a glum expression – in supermarkets for instance? So many look so harassed.

Sally: The world is too much with us late and soon,
Getting and spending we lay waste our powers' [5]

Peter: Is 'spirit' the same as 'soul'? We talk about 'the spirit of the game' – or, as the Western Brothers sang, 'play the game, you cads, play the game'! Equally as important as the rules of the game is the spirit of the game.

Sally: Music is the voice of the spirit, art is its handmaiden, human love its tender fulfilment.

Peter: Then what is the difference between soul and spirit?

Sally: The soul is the spirit healed by the word of God. The gospel elevates the spirit of a person. Awake to God, his soul awakens too, in a union of body, brain, spirit.

Peter: Everything he can hope to know about himself at that point you would say?

---

[3] Mark 8:36-7   [5] William Worsdworth
[4] Mark 12:30

Sally: Our Lord prayed in the Garden of Gethsemane on the night of his betrayal:

'My soul is exceeding sorrowful even unto death' [6]

Peter: I think that Christ's whole being was in that cry.

Sally: The total man was in agony – body, mind, spirit.

Peter: I heard one of our people greet another last Sunday, 'All well with your soul?'

Sally:
(sings softly)

When peace like a river attendeth my way,
When sorrows like sea-billows roll,
Whatever my lot, thou hast taught me to know
It is well, it is well with my soul. [7]

Is it well with your soul, Peter?

Peter: I thank God, yes, but I want to ask something else. What does 'resurrection' mean?

Sally: The victory of Christ over death is the very heart of the gospel. Christians are resurrection people.

Peter: Does that mean 'Dem dry bones' coming together again? Like in the negro spiritual?

Sally: Ezekiel had a dream of a graveyard bursting into new life – into resurrection.

Peter: Who was Ezekiel?

Sally: An early-day Hebrew prophet. His nation had been conquered and carried into exile. Ezekiel had this extraordinary dream of the nation's liberation and restoration – a perfect picture of resurrection.

Peter: 'Thigh bone to hip bone' — I remember the song; then whole skeletons joined up, then sinew and muscle on the skeletons. Was the resurrection of Jesus Christ like that?

Sally: On Easter day we sing

Up from the grave he arose
With a mighty triumph o'er his foes. [8]

---

[6] Mark 14:34

[7] *SASB* 771

[8] *SASB* 148

Peter: And Christ's bones came together like the spiritual says?

Sally: It's a mystery, Peter, and St. Paul wrote that if he knew all mysteries and didn't have love for people, he would still know nothing. [9]

Peter: I find this idea of a body coming alive again very, very difficult indeed. Wasn't there a Bishop who caused a furore when he said that the resurrected Christ was about much more than tricks with bones? Don't you think that the resurrection of Jesus is the victory of his spirit of love over the hatred of those who killed him. He prayed for them from his cross. 'Father forgive them for they don't know what they are doing'? [10]

Sally: The gospels give us several word pictures of the risen Christ making himself known. For instance, read John's Gospel, chapter 20.

Peter: I have.

A woman who loved Christ dearly saw him in the face and figure of an ordinary working man.

Sally: Read Luke 24.

Peter: I have.

Two country people eat supper together in the peace and calm of their cottage. As they talk together, they relive the friendship with Jesus of the past days and months, and he becomes vividly alive for them again. Love is stronger than death. These two people were overwhelmed by their love for their Lord and his love for them.

Sally: Read John 20 verse 19.

Peter: I have.

Directors of a limited liability company call a board meeting. Business is bad. Liquidation seems inevitable. Then they remember who founded their company. They drink a toast to him and the secretary rewrites the agenda. The future is bright once more.

---

[9] 1 Corinthians 13:2   [10] Luke 23:34

Sally: Read John 21.

Peter: I have.

After drawing a blank all night a fishing crew strike rich, two boats are weighed down with fish. Overcome with amazement one fisherman said to another 'the Lord is here'. Their Lord and Master was still with them.

Sally: That was the disciple John, speaking to Peter. Well then, read 1 Corinthians 15:6.

Peter: I have.

A believers' rally of some 500 people of all ages came together to remember Jesus and to mourn for his cruel death. Suddenly the spirit of doom and gloom lifts … A solemn liturgy becomes a Salvation Army rally. I love it! The love of Christ lit up every heart, in renewed resurrection life.

Sally: Jesus said, 'I am the resurrection and the life, he that believes in me though he were dead yet shall he live'. [11]

Peter: But don't you think he meant rather more than 'dem bones'?

Sally: Here is a paragraph I copied from a book by A.M. Ramsey, sometime Archbishop of Canterbury:

> Thus if the resurrection is pointing us towards a miracle we will not be troubled, for a miracle will mean not only a breach of the laws that have been perceived in this world but a manifestation of the purpose of the Creator of a new world and the redeemer of our own. And if the evidence is pointing us toward an act wherein spirit and body are strangely blended and exalted our minds will have no terrors; for the message of the New Testament is pervaded through and through by the belief that the spiritual and the material are interwoven in the purpose of the word-made-flesh. Why is it judged incredible with you if God should raise the dead? [12]

[11] John 11:25
[12] *The Resurrection of Christ* pp.56,57

Peter: Lo, a new creation dawning!
Lo I rise to life divine!
In my soul an Easter morning;
I am Christ's and Christ is mine[13]

Major, would it be all right were I to say that that verse expresses all that I can understand of Christ's resurrection? His love was more powerful than his enemies' hatred. His spirit did not perish. He entrusted it to God when he cried from the cross, 'Father, into your hands, I commend my spirit'[14] and his loving spirit has flowed out into the whole of life and especially into his Church. My heart overflowed with his love when I knelt at the Mercy Seat. I now see the risen Christ in every simple act of human kindness.

Sally: Jesus said that to believe in him was to have eternal life.[15]

Peter: Many people look on death as a door marked 'Exit', a final step.

Sally: Christians take the first step into a new form of life – spirit and body interwoven, as Ramsey put it.

Peter: You Salvationists describe death as promotion to Glory. Do you not know sorrow sometimes?

Sally: The death of a child, or death from a tragic accident, untimely death of any kind – the death of soldiers and civilians in Iraq, for instance — always brings deep, deep sorrow. Commissioner Kathleen Kendrick used to say 'If you want to understand The Salvation Army come to a Salvation Army funeral'. She knew that her own service would overflow with thanksgiving to God for his mercy and truth.

Peter: No sadness, ever?

Sally: I know a widower, married to his wife for 60 years, who says that life is now 'a lengthening and a longing'.

---

[13] *SASB* 520
[14] Luke 23:46
[15] John 3:15

Peter: To live on in the hearts of those you love is not to die.

Sally: Richard Chartres, Bishop of London, has written, 'The Christian faith is a constant struggle against death'.[16]

Peter: In time of war people say, 'God is nowhere'.

Sally: Say rather, God is now here. 'Woodbine Willie' (Military Chaplain, Rev. Studdert Kennedy) surrounded by the carnage of the trenches in World War I, wrote:

> So the Father God goes sorrowing still.
>> For 'Is world what 'as gone to sea,
> But 'E runs up a light on Calvary's 'eight
>> That beckons to you and me.
> The beacon light of the sorrow of God
>> 'As been shinin' down through the years.
> A-flashin' its light through the darkest night,
>> O' our 'uman blood and tears'[17]

Peter: I believe in life beyond life and I see the life of the Risen Christ in every simple act of kindness.

Recently I was travelling back to London by train after a few days holiday in lovely Dorset. It seemed the right use of time to pen my 'thank you' note to my host and hostess while I travelled. I could then post the note on arrival at Waterloo. I knew I had postage stamps. I didn't know that I had no envelope.

Seated in the opposite corner from me, busily working at his papers, was a railway official. Much daring, I approached him. Had he an unused envelope he could spare? He hunted through his papers and briefcase. No envelope. I thanked him for his trouble and returned to my seat. I then noticed his mobile phone was in his hand. 'I have telephoned Winchester Station' he said. 'They will have an envelope brought to you when we arrive in 7 minutes'. It was there!

---

[16] *The War Cry* 12 November 2005
[17] *The Unutterable Beauty*, p.134

Sally: I think that man must have been a Christian, Peter.

Peter: You miss my point, Major. I don't think he necessarily was. I posted my letter at Waterloo. I believe he would have posted it for me had I asked him.

Sally: Paul wrote: 'For me to live is Christ and to die is gain'.[18]

Peter: But where is heaven, not beyond the blue horizon surely?

Sally: At the last supper Jesus, 'knowing that he was come from God and went to God' brought heaven to earth by becoming cloak room attendant for his disciples.

Peter: We come from God and we go to God, life beyond life. That says it all for me. But what about the Kingdom of Heaven?

Sally: Matthew's gospel looks forward to the setting up of the Kingdom of Heaven.

Peter: It's part of the Lord's Prayer – 'For yours is the Kingdom, the power and the glory for ever'

Sally: Christ's promise to his disciples was:

'I appoint unto you a Kingdom . . .'[19]

The Kingdom of Heaven is an alternative way of speaking of God's righteous rule. The writers of Matthew's gospel were reluctant to write God's name as it was too holy to be written.

Peter: But the Kingdom of Heaven is not mentioned in the doctrines. That's something else the General might look at, isn't it?

Sally: When you sign your articles of war you agree to make the values of the Kingdom and not the values of the world your standard for life.

Peter: The Kingdom of Heaven – God's righteous rule – will become a reality when Christ's spirit of love rules in the world, not when any country proves that it has one

---

[18] Philippians: 1:21
[19] John 13:3

nuclear warhead more than any other country – God forbid. God's world desperately needs saving, needs the salvation of Jesus — the man for others like no man before him nor any man since — Jesus, son of man.

Sally: And Son of God, otherwise heaven is impossible to conceive.

Peter: So we furnish it with golden harps and pearly gates. Heaven becomes real when people try to make good things happen for other people who cannot make them happen for themselves. If I understand correctly, that was our Lord's announced manifesto in the synagogue in Nazareth.[21]

Sally: And that is what Matthew 25 is all about.

Peter: And what the Army is all about, too, which is why I want to be a soldier in its ranks, despite my problem with 'dem bones'!

Sally: Something seems to have caught your eye, Peter. What are you staring at?

Peter: That high-rise office block we can see from where we are standing. There's something familiar about it, what is it?

Sally: You'll have seen it in the background on the news or in discussion programmes about asylum. It's the government's immigration centre. All asylum seekers make application there.

Peter: Then do you think we could spend a few minutes in the meeting hall? I would like to pray for that place, and particularly for the staff with their difficult responsibilities. May they be patient with every applicant and treat each person with respect.

Sally: The Nazareth manifesto.
We'll pray together, Peter.

---

[20] Luke 4:18

On Location
in Whitechapel
Son of God, Son of Man

WE LAST caught up with Major Sally Storey and Peter some weeks ago in Croydon, south London. Today we are in east London with them, in original Booth territory.

Whitechapel Road is a busy highway - so no parking. They travelled by bus to New Cross Station, then on the Whitechapel and City tube to Whitechapel Station. Booth House is hardly more than one hundred yards from the station.

In anticipation of the visit Sally had secured a copy of *With Booth in London*, a fascinating study written by the late Lieut-Colonel Cyril Barnes, well-known SA historian — still available from Salvationist Publishing and Supplies.

> Outside the Blind Beggar public house, a few yards west of Mile End Gate, now demolished, stood a group of missioners preaching the gospel. Booth stopped, listened and immediately felt an affinity with the speakers …
>
> The leader of the meeting asked Booth if he would like to 'have a word'. He responded gladly.
>
> Within moments passers-by were attracted from all directions. Here was a man who understood them and used words they knew … While Booth spoke the missioners stood transfixed
>
> 'This is the leader we want at the tent' they exclaimed to each other … Thus on Sunday 2 July 1865 Booth conducted a service out of which grew the international Salvation Army. In that first meeting between 200 and 300 people, most of them poorly dressed and unkempt, sat on wooden benches in an unventilated tent where the only illumination was from suspended swinging, hissing naphtha lamps …

Selected from *With Booth in London*, Cyril Barnes, p.14

Aftersight and Foresight (7)

We believe that in the person of Jesus Christ the Divine and human natures are united, so that he is truly and properly God and truly and properly man.

Doctrine 4

SALLY: Here we are in Booth House, Whitechapel Road, one of 45 such hostels in the United Kingdom and Republic of Ireland. Booth House was opened by Her Majesty The Queen in 1968 and has recently been extensively upgraded.

Peter: How many men are housed here?

Sally: About 150; nationwide some 3,000. The doss house days have long since gone. Booth House is a resettlement centre, not a warehouse. Every guest works through a personal rehabilitation programme. The men live in clusters of ten when they join the programme; each man is allotted his individual room but shares facilities. Men graduate through the programme to individual self-contained apartments. Majors Julian and Hilarie Watchorn are the joint managers. Local authorities help with funding.

Peter: This is Booth territory, isn't it?

Sally: We are just half a mile east of the Blind Beggar public house outside of which Booth came upon a group of missioners conducting a gospel meeting.

The year was 1865. The date, Sunday July 2nd, Booth 'joined up' on the spot, and accepted their invitation to stay with them as their leader. Until recently, just along the road from here was a sundial, unveiled by Commr Catherine Bramwell-Booth, marking the spot where the

56

tent was pitched in which Booth conducted his first indoor meeting. Here at Booth House, we are but a stone's throw from the site on which stood the house which he made his first headquarters.

Riverside House is also close, just by West India Dock gates. This upgraded facility, opened on 12 December 2005, provides accommodation for 60 homeless men grappling with substance misuse, 40 in self.-catering clusters, and 20 in self-contained one bedroom flats. All residents will be expected to be drug and alcohol free and will be supported in maintaining an abstinent lifestyle. Referrals will come from those who have already completed detox or rehab programmes, those being discharged from prison or those in existing hostels who will benefit from a 'dry' environment.

Peter: Society is comfortable only with 'normal' people. It views abnormality with suspicion. That's why mental illness can become a music hall joke, and why we have not found an alternative to prison for criminal abnormality.

Sally: The Army is not put off by abnormality. 'Whosoever will may come...' — and 60 men slept warmly under the Riverside roof last night.

Peter: Sleep that knits up the ravell'd sleeve of care,
        The death of each day's life, sore labour's bath,
        Balm of hurt minds, great nature's second course,
        Chief nourisher in life's feast.

Macbeth, Act 2

Whitechapel is Booth Country right enough. That sundial heralded the dawn of hope for all the world.

Sally: Booth's mission crossed the Atlantic to the USA in 1880, then to France, followed by Canada, India, soon afterwards Switzerland. The flag flies in 111 countries today. Jesus gave his disciples a commission 'Go into all the world and teach all nations' … Booth said, 'my arms are around the world and my heart is set on its salvation'.

Peter: A fine sentiment and a fine sentence – fourteen words, twelve of them of one syllable.

Sally: More than a sentiment, Peter, and I doubt whether Booth was aware he was using words of one syllable. His language was always the simplest possible. His son Bramwell, our second General, said, 'The Salvation Army is love for souls'.

Peter: But respect for the person, genuine interest in the other fellow, comes first surely? If I were drowning in a river I would rather see on the riverbank a burglar who could swim, than a bishop who couldn't.

Sally: Commissioner Koshi Hasegawa, former Territorial Commander of Japan, combined respect for the person with love for his soul.

Not long after her husband's promotion to Glory in 1970 Mrs Hasegawa sat turning the pages of his Bible. Among the leaves was a piece of paper. She unfolded it. It was headed 'My Will'. She read it carefully.

A right relationship to God and our fellow men,' she read, 'To parents and children, brothers and sisters, husband and wife, superior officers and assisting officers, colleagues and comrades.

The right relationship to those in our care: love them, lead them, make every effort for them; shed your tears for them many times. We are called to do it, we stake our lives upon it'.

The document finished with: 'Take your share of suffering as a good soldier of Christ Jesus. Preach the word, be urgent in season and out of season, convince, rebuke and exhort, be unfailing in patience and in teaching'.

Hasegawa's 'will' was to do the will of God. He had a burning desire that his countrymen should do the same. Mrs Hasegawa, knew this, so in her usual practical way had 'the will' copied and sent to officers and soldiers alike that they might have a share in the 'will' and help to build God's kingdom of love and peace in Japan.

Peter: A remarkable last will and testament.

Sally: Jesus said, 'the good shepherd gives his life for the sheep'.[1]

Peter: I loved to recite when I was a kid, 'foxes have holes, birds of the air have nests, but the son of man has nowhere to lay his head'![2] Another splendid sentence — 20 words, 18 of them one syllable.

Sally: Son of God, son of man, conceived by the Holy Spirit, born of the Virgin Mary as the angel Gabriel told Mary her son would be.

Peter: Angel Gabriel? Do angels have names?

Sally: God's messenger reveals himself by the name of Gabriel because that was the name by which he was commonly known among the Jews.

Peter: Virgin birth? Jesus born of a virgin? 'Virgin' could be read as 'young maiden' couldn't it? or 'a girl promised in marriage'.

Sally: We believe in the virgin birth, Peter.

Peter: But it isn't in our doctrines, you know. And Paul never mentions it in any of his letters to young Christians so far as I am aware.

Sally: *Salvation Story* says 'Jesus' personal life and character cannot be explained solely in terms of human heredity. God was at work in Jesus from the moment of his conception'.

Peter: 'God was at work in Jesus from the moment of his conception' … I have absolutely no problem with that.

Sally: If the virgin birth is not included in our doctrines it is because the truth was universally accepted among believers. There was no need to include it among our special emphases. I do not analyse like you Peter, I accept the mystery of the gospel.

---

[1] John 10:11
[2] Luke 9:58

Peter: And so do I, especially the unique manhood of Jesus – the man for others like no other before him nor any man since. Catholics name Mary as mother of God, don't they?

Sally: Salvationists don't.

Peter: Why not – if Jesus was the son of God and Mary was his mother?

Sally: Mary was a mother *for* God.

Peter: Like no other mother before her nor any mother since.

Sally: Mother for every mother watching over a sick child.

Peter: Mother for every mother queuing for water at a stand-pipe.

Sally: Mother for every wife, daughter and mother fearing news from Iraq. Mother for every teenage girl loitering at the kerbside, hoping, hoping …

Peter: And weeping into her pillow that night because she still hasn't enough to pay the rent.

Sally: Jesus cried from his cross, 'Mother behold your son'.[3]

Peter: Perhaps we can think of Mary crying 'Son – sons all of you – remember my daughters'.

Sally: Perhaps I should talk more often about Mary, mother *for* God, woman for all women.

Peter: Not only on Mother's Day.

Sally: Probably the family lived in one room. Jesus had four brothers and at least two sisters. There was no spare money, and in that home he would have learned the give and take of family life.

Mary would have taught him the equivalent of 'Lord keep us safe this night' — Psalm 31:5, 'Into thy hands I commit my spirit' — and every Sabbath she would have taken him to sit with her in the women's section of the synagogue.[4]

---

[3] John 19:26
[4] Matthew 13:55,56

Here is a moving Mother's Day story for you:

Will Cooper left school when he was thirteen years old and his mum died a year later. Will's Dad faithfully soldiered on but family life could not have been easy. During World War I, Will was in mine-sweepers on the North Sea. Many years later, Will, by now a Salvation Army Officer himself and Territorial Commander for Denmark, wrote an article for *The War Cry* which was a response to a previous article that had appeared about his Mum.

TWO SURPRISED SERVICEMEN

During the First World War I enlisted in the RNVR and was trained at the Crystal Palace. I attended the Penge Corps. On the Sunday morning of Mother's Day the late Mrs Colonel Thomas Lewis asked me to represent the navy boys and pay a tribute to my mother in the night meeting. This was an ordeal, for I had only recently visited mother's grave for the first time since the funeral and I was feeling the loss most keenly. However, I did speak, broke down and the large congregation wept with me. Following me was an elderly man, who was speaking on behalf of the men of the army. He said that he could not speak about his real mother, for drink and debauchery were his only memory of her, but he would say something about his spiritual mother. He then described the woman who had led him to Christ — the Army Captain at a Suffolk corps.

She had mended his clothes, protected him from wrong friendships and loved him into discipleship. He said that her name was Captain Fairhurst. Immediately Mrs Colonel Lewis grasped the situation and said to the congregation: "Unknown to each other, these two men are talking about the same woman - the mother of the navy lad is the spiritual mother of the soldier."

There was no address that night and the Mercy Seat was filled many times.

Peter: Jesus' favoured name for himself was son of man – the Christ of the human road. Sing it for me again, Major you have a beautiful voice.

Sally:
(sings softly)

> He's the Christ of the human road
>   And he offers to carry our load;
> He's walking our way, ev'ry night, ev'ry day,
>   This Christ of the human road.
> He is human and yet so divine,
> And he knows your heart's sorrow and mine.
> In all times of need, he's a true friend indeed,
>   This Christ of the human road.

(George Bennard)

Peter: Mary, mother of the son of man, the man for others.

> If Jesus Christ is a man;
>   And only a man, — I say
> That of all mankind I cleave to him,
>   And to him I will cleave alway.
> If Jesus Christ is a God,
>   And the only God, — I swear
> I will follow Him through heaven and hell,
>   The earth, the sea, and the air.

Sally: Who wrote that?

Peter: Richard Watson Gilder. He called his lines 'The Song of a Heathen'. I also like John Drinkwater's piece:

> Shakespeare is dust and will not come
> To question from his Avon tomb,
> And Socrates and Shelley keep
> An Attic and Italian sleep.
>
> They see not! But, O Christians who
> Throng Holborn and Fifth Avenue,
> May we not meet, in spite of death,
> A traveller from Nazareth?'

Sally: Then how does Jesus Christ save, Peter? You have received him as your Saviour.

Peter: Jesus Christ of Nazareth saves men and women from their sins by the strength of his love. He draws us to himself, out from the mists of our self-will and self-approval by achieving the impossible — he embraces us with love which is stronger than our self-love.

Sally: But God's righteous love had to be satisfied, and his righteous wrath appeased. The penalty for sin had to be paid. Jesus was the one and only full and complete sacrifice for sin. His death atoned for the sins of the whole world. He redeemed us by accepting the penalty for sin on our behalf.

Peter: You are using words, Major - precious to you, and to many like you, but with little meaning for me. He redeemed me with his love, Major, not by doctrine or dogma. For me Jesus Christ of Nazareth is God's son because he was son of man, the man for others like no other man before him nor any man since.

Sally: You puzzle me, Peter. I am confused. St Paul uses these images to teach us about Christ as Saviour — Christ a living sacrifice accepted by God to appease his righteous wrath because of our sinning. Isaac Watts wrote:

> Not all the blood of beasts
> On Jewish altars slain
> Could give the guilty conscience peace,
> Or wash away our stain.
>
> But Christ, the heavenly Lamb
> Takes all our sins away,
> A sacrifice of nobler name
> And richer blood than they.

(*SASB* 120)

Peter: Don't be confused, Major. Words can confuse. They can be great sinners. You are using words, Major, precious to you and to Isaac Watts (and who am I to tangle with that giant?) but with little meaning for me. Paul was saved by love, wasn't he? Not by such religious theories as you have suggested. Jesus Christ did not appease God's wrath. What kind of God would he be if so?

Sally: Paul saved by love — how do you mean?

Peter: Paul was present in Jerusalem at the execution of Stephen, the first Christian martyr. Acts 7:58-60 describes Stephen's death. 'And they stoned Stephen . . . calling upon God, and saying, Lord, lay not this sin to their charge'.

Sally: An echo of Christ's prayer from the cross concerning his executioners, 'Father forgive them, for they don't know what they are doing'

Peter: Right. I think Stephen's spirit of love and his prayer of forgiveness for his persecutors in the name of Christ got to Paul and marked his spiritual awakening. He surely said to himself, 'If there is true religious faith anywhere, this is it. This disciple of Christ, Stephen, is praying even for these misguided men who are savaging his broken body.'

Sally: But later, in his teaching as an apostle of Christ Paul used all those words which you say have little meaning for you.

Peter: I think the explanation is simply this. Paul could not escape from the teaching received in his youth, and perhaps did not wish to do so. As a boy and as a youth he had been soaked in the ancient Hebrew culture, where forgiveness for sin and the worship of Jehovah required the shedding of blood in a sacrifice on an altar.

This misguided notion was totally ingrained in him. Moreover, he was by no means ashamed of his Hebrew upbringing, rather was it his proud boast, 'I am a Pharisee, the son of a Pharisee.'

And as for me — even though all the divinity schools in Christendom may continue to recite the dogma of Christ as a sacrifice for human sinfulness it still does not make it true.

Sally: I don't suppose anybody ever totally escapes from the indoctrination of their childhood.

Peter: Along Damascus Rd. and onwards this was now Paul's dilemma. He wanted to accept Stephen's grasp of true religion to be love and only love, love all the way, love to the end, but this new awakening would need to blend with old religious thought-forms. And so he dragged into his new life with Christ all the apparatus of ancient Jewry, its full sacrificial order.

Sally: Not all, not that business of circumcision or of dietary laws. And think of all those inspiring hymns which have been written about the atonement made by Christ.

Peter: I sing them with all my heart, especially Isaac Watts' inspiring hymns. But there is one verse which for me says everything. I believe the words were written by General Orsborn:

> With an everlasting love, He lovèd us,
>   O wonderful, O merciful!
> Never was there manifest such love before!
>   We can never tell the depths of agony
> And suffering He bore,
>   But we know He died for love of us —
> And he could not do more.

Sally: I believe that, too

Peter: We both believe the same truth, Major.

Sally: I believe in the virgin birth.

Peter: God was at work in Jesus from the moment of his conception.

Sally: Time we were on our way, Peter, though just a moment — I am sure you feel as inspired as I do, standing here near the spot in that old Quaker burial ground where the marquee was pitched in which William Booth preached to 'a few desolate souls'. It is the birthplace of The Salvation Army.

Peter: I find myself deeply moved, Major

Sally: Now would you like to stretch your legs and walk three or four hundred yards to look in on Hopetown?

Peter: Hopetown? What a fascinating name. What is Hopetown?

Sally: A state of the art expression of the sixth doctrine —

Peter: We believe that the Lord Jesus Christ has, by his suffering and death, made an atonement for the whole world so that whosoever will may be saved. I know it, you see!

Sally: Hopetown has 108 family rooms for homeless women, with shared kitchen and lounge facilities. A drop-in centre on the ground floor will be supervised by the local health authority, offering counsel for drug-dependent women.

Peter: A brand-new facility in the same caring Booth spirit.

Sally: Right on the second count, but not new-new. Be very careful crossing this busy road. We go past Booth House, turn right here at the petrol station into Devren Street. Hopetown is straight ahead in Old Montague Street.

Peter: Hopetown not a new facility, you say?

Sally: Major David Pickard is Hopetown's Administrator. He will tell you the Hopetown story. I have him on my mobile. I'm passing you over, Peter, to my friend Major Pickard.

HISTORY OF HOPETOWN

THE OPENING of the new Hopetown Centre in 2006 is a significant milestone in the history of The Salvation Army. Situated in Whitechapel, in the East End of London, it is a continuation, in very modern surroundings, of a work first begun in that area in 1884, and it is to that work that Hopetown is able to trace its origins. People starved to death on the streets of London in the 1880's, and many women and young girls were faced with prostitution as the only alternative to starvation.

Early-day Salvationists took such girls into their own homes, the best-known of these being Mrs. Cotterill, who patrolled the streets of Whitechapel at night seeking girls in need of help, and took them to her own home. It took great courage for her to do this, as often she suffered violence from men who sought the girls for a very different purpose.

The time came when her own home could take no more, and her husband's protestations grew ever more urgent. The need for a refuge for homeless women was established and on May 22, 1884 a small house in Hanbury Street, Whitechapel was rented for the purpose, and filled immediately. This work grew apace, and Mrs. Bramwell Booth was asked to take charge. It was thought essential that the girls and women should be able to earn an honest living upon leaving the Army's care, and so from the earliest days training was given in housewifery, cooking, needlework and laundry work. Preparing residents for independent living beyond hostel life is not exactly a new idea!

In 1929 The Salvation Army purchased a derelict school in Finch Street, Whitechapel. With skill, hard work and ingenuity it was transformed into a new home for women previously housed in the Hanbury Street Shelter. On Wednesday 16 December 1931, Her Majesty Queen Mary officially opened the renovated building, aptly naming it 'Hope Town', for it not only provided accommodation for 300 women and a number of children, but also gave them hope.

The necessary renovations and reconstruction, when added to the purchase price, had brought the total cost to

£32,000. Lord Rothermere headed the subscription list with £5,000. City banks and companies contributed £1,500 and Queen Mary undertook to provide a cubicle. Finch Street was re-named Hope Town Street by order of the London County Council on 1 January. 1939.

But the home's dedicated caring and rehabilitation work was abruptly halted when the building was severely destroyed by bombing in November 1940, and it remained closed for eight years. Meantime, hundreds of homeless women and children were cared for in temporary accommodation at Clapton. In November 1948, following extensive repairs, Hope Town enjoyed another day of great celebration when it was reopened by Her Royal Highness the Duchess of Gloucester. Queen Mary sent an assurance of her continued interest and a photograph of herself to replace the one lost in the air-raid.

Hope Town II was born, and for more than 30 years it continued to meet the needs of homeless women. Further progress came in 1980 when, following demolition and rebuilding, a new, much more modern centre for homeless women was brought into being. Hopetown III was opened by Her Majesty Queen Elizabeth II, in Old Montague Street. But progress is unrelenting, and by 2004 the need for a much more modern building was apparent. The demolition men once again moved into Old Montague Street.

Now, The Salvation Army proudly presents Hopetown IV, a state-of-the-art residential centre fit for the 21st century. When Her Majesty Queen Mary opened the first Hopetown, she expressed the earnest hope that 'sunshine and blessing' would be brought into the lives of the homeless, friendless women who came through the doors.

This hope still continues in the new Hopetown . . .

Sally: Thank you David, we have to make our way home now. It has been quite a long day for Peter and me.

Peter: But such an interesting day, Major, and so informative. The visit to Hopetown has crowned the day. I have enjoyed every moment. Thank you for every arrangement.

Sally: Back to Whitechapel Station and home!

On Location
with Booth and Barnardo
in Hope Place
The Boy is Father of the Man

A WEEK OR SO later the two researchers repeated the Blackheath, New Cross, Whitechapel journey. Peter had picked up the story of William Booth's encounter with Dr. Barnardo and wanted to know more.

Major Sally thought it a useful idea to take a look at the Royal London Hospital, Whitechapel, directly opposite Booth House.

The young Barnardo had been a medical student at 'the London'.

> Seeing the Christian Mission operating at the street corners Barnardo, a student at the London Hospital (in Whitechapel Road) threw himself into the work and helped the Missioners … one evening Barnardo told William Booth of his intention to do something for homeless boys. And that he had taken a house to begin in. 'Where is it?' asked Booth. 'Hope Place, Bull Lane, Stepney' was the reply. 'What is the rent?' 'Eight shillings for the downstairs, and we shall get the upstairs which is another four shillings'.
>
> They shook hands and parted with mutual expressions of thanks and wishes for each other's success.

> *History of The Salvation Army* Volume I, p.111
> – Robert Sandall

Distinctive red tents supplied by The Salvation Army in Pakistan following the earthquake of 8 October 2005.

The children below love the camera, but you'd never believe how cold it was!

See pages16ff.

A carefully monitored project board helps The Salvation Army and others to organise rebuilding of damaged houses in the Andaman Islands.

And on the Indian mainland every sinew is strained as one of the many fishing boats provided by The Salvation Army International Development comes ashore

See pages 12ff.

Absolute attention on the teacher, in this Salvation Army Tsunami Response Education Centre, (see opposite page) but what young pupil anywhere can resist a wave at the camera?

Above:

This former 'adult' shop is now *Nicely Saved*. Where once seedy 'XXX' signs were displayed The Salvation Army, with help from other churches in Stapleford, offers a utility serving the whole community.

Salvationist 19 August 2006

Right:

Jake and Jez Thomas present bouquets to newly-elected General Shaw Clifton and Commr Helen Clifton at Sunbury Court

See pages 5 and 71 — also
www.salvationarmy.org.uk/salvationist

Left:

Derek Foster MP, with Major Nigel Bovey, editor of *The War Cry* in the Speaker's apartments, House of Commons, 1996

See page 93

Above:

Canadian Record sleeve
John Gowans with cast of *Glory!*
John Larsson, signed souvenir

The Princess Royal talks with General John Larsson and Major
Charles Swansbury at the opening of the new IHQ building

See pages 12, 77 and 112

Below:

A record number of delegates attended the 5th Music Leaders Training Seminar
at Park Road Conference Centre in Nairobi See page 71

Above:
This Congress Hall postcard from the early 1900s shows that 'Cinematograph' was used to attract crowds. The Salvation Army has always used modern methods!

Right:
Platform scene, 19 March 1931 inside the auditorium

Above:
The cadets assemble ready to march into Clapton and beyond

Right:
London Orphan Asylum

See pages 87ff.

©Brady & Mallalieu

Above:
   The scene today

Left:
   The Clapton Portico learning centre

Below:
   Inside the new structure

©Brady & Mallalieu

Below:
   Imposing ancient columns, practical modern lift

©Brady & Mallalieu

Commissioner Robin Dunster, first woman Chief of
Staff of The Salvation Army chats to the Lord Mayor
— see below and page 12

LORD MAYOR OF LONDON, Alderman David Brewer CMG, unveiled a plaque
at International Headquarters, recognising a New City Architecture Award by the
Worshipful Company of Chartered Architects. The Lord Mayor described the
building as a 'trophy of grace' which 'proclaims the living gospel'
Salvationist 12 August 2006

Aftersight and Foresight (8)

We believe that we are justified by grace through faith in our Lord Jesus Christ and that he that believeth hath the witness in himself.

Doctrine 8

PETER: I'm sorry to keep rabbiting on Major, but what does 'justified' mean? And why 'believeth' and 'hath'? Are these forms of speech further evidence of an 1838 carry-over?

Sally: The language of the doctrine may be old-fashioned, but the Army's mission is bang up-to-date. Retired General John Larsson called the world-wide Army to - 'A Year for Children and Youth' in 2005

Peter: Winning the interest of children in the gospel gets more and more difficult I suppose. 24/7 TV, outings in the family car at weekends, and so on.

Sally: Salvationist Olive Sell of Ware Corps remembers her service in the THQ Youth Department forty years ago. She writes:

> It all seemed so easy then. We knew what we wanted and the way forward seemed clear – we just had to provide the energy. It is very different today!

Peter: Tell me about ALOVE.

Sally: In 2004 the Territory launched ALOVE, an intriguing sub-brand. Director Russell Rook says: 'Same Army, next generation!'

Peter: An off-shoot?

Sally: Say, rather, an input. ALOVE creates training programmes for new youth leaders for instance. However, ALOVE does not encourage its youthful enthusiasts to wear Salvation Army uniform. The thought is that 'civvies' make outreach to other young people easier. Only time will tell if they are right.

Peter: Two men out of three wear tee shirts proudly displaying the name of their favourite soccer team or favourite tipple. Was 'A Year for Children and Youth' a success?

Sally: *Salvationist* reported that in the United Kingdom and the Republic of Ireland attendance at our youth events increased by 54 per cent.

Peter: Thanks to ALOVE.

Sally: Yes, and to the Children's Ministries Unit at THQ headed by Major Roger Batt.

Peter: What about overseas?

Sally: The USA Central Territory increased its Junior Soldiers' strength by 42 per cent comparing January to May 2004 with the same period in 2005.

The Australian Southern Territory produced a Prayer Focus Resource book and every corps mobilised itself to pray for children and youth. These are just two examples of world-wide initiative.

Peter: What about the future?

Sally: Our young people are the Army of today and for tomorrow. Jake and Jez Thomas, Junior Soldiers of Staines Corps presented a bouquet of flowers to General Shaw and Commr Helen Clifton at Sunbury Court. Jake and Jez were representing more than 350,000 Junior Soldiers world-wide[1].

Bristol Easton Corps, in association with British Airways, mounted a music school for some 90 young Kenyan Salvationists[2].

---

[1] See colour plates
[2] See colour plates

Some of the students travelled for days to get to Thika, to our high school for visually handicapped young adults in Kenya, which was the venue for the music school.

Peter: Does the Army have all-the-year-round schools?

Sally: Major Christine Clement writes:

> Throughout the world The Salvation Army maintains almost 2000 schools … As the Deputy Director of UNICEF commented … "Education is the best investment we can make".

Peter: And in the UK?

Sally: At Weston-Super-Mare 400 pupils from Walliscote School attended Assembly in the corps hall. Major Keith Wallis, the Corps Officer – no, the school is not named after him! – explained the flag and what Salvationists believe.

Peter: Anything else?

Sally: Naomi Pountain, a Salvationist of Falkirk Corps, a student teacher, visited Uganda during her summer holiday. Children affected by HIV/Aids are often left uneducated. Naomi felt she should raise money for the education of some she met. Men and women on community service who visit Falkirk Corps Community Café raised £100 and Salvationist Irene Lumsden raised £50 with a cake sale.

Peter: Splendid initiative.

Sally: Our corps at Clapton, thriving progeny of the old Congress Hall [3] is experiencing a truly remarkable awakening. Recently, the first prize-giving for a number of years included the presentation of more than 20 Bibles on Children's Sunday.

Our Music Ministries Unit at THQ, working with Major Noreen Batt of the Children's Ministries Unit has

[3] See colour plates

launched *Sing to the Lord,* a resource book of musical activities easily adaptable for Sunday schools.

Peter: What about *Kids Alive*?

Sally: Superb – the only weekly Christian comic published by any church in the UK, choc-a-bloc with interest, with features designed for kids of all ages (including mums and dads). I never cease to be amazed at the ability of the editor and his production team to meet their weekly deadline, 'not somehow but triumphantly'. The technology involved – *Kids Alive* is 100 per cent colour – is staggering.

Peter: I wonder if UK Salvationists appreciate the paper as they should? Do they push it as they might? – And your other weeklies, *The War Cry,* and *Salvationist.*

In all the years I have been away from the Army a Salvationist friend has passed his copies of *Salvationist* on to me.

Sally: Our literary and editorial teams are totally dedicated to salvationist mission.

Peter: With such high professional standards, too.

Sally: Every issue of *The War Cry* communicates with the man in the street in quite brilliant fashion. You won't find a glib word on any page. Flinty thinking combined with hard writing make for easy reading. For instance, when George Best died last year and the media hailed that brilliant footballer with an enthusiasm amounting almost to idolatry —

Peter: Belfast airport has now been named after him. George was a genius.

Sally: — I am hardly a soccer fan but I always found Georgie-boy exciting to watch on the telly. However, there was a sad downside. Booze proved to be no friend to George.

The War Cry of 3 December 2005 added its own voice to the nationwide chorus of praise for the lad from

Belfast and then, deftly, delicately pointed out that alcohol is a highly addictive drug that is one of the UK's biggest killers with some 38,000 deaths a year besides being the cause of tens of thousands of alcohol-related injuries.

Booze doesn't choose.

It is no respecter of persons. It can ruin anyone. Even the best.

Peter: *Salvationist* vibrates with pages of Salvation Army news, presented in exciting style, with an abundance of photographs and illustrations, professional journalism with love at its heart

Sally: A UK weekly (like *The War Cry*) read eagerly all over the world.

Captain Sheila Dunkinson, a British officer who is serving in Singapore wrote recently:

> I regularly read *Salvationist* from cover to cover with the attention to detail which is possibly found only in reinforcement officers far away from home.'

Sally: And the Schools and Colleges Information Service at THQ – the key department for providing resources for teachers and students studying the Army has recently produced two new colour booklets for use in schools.

Peter: Only the best is good enough for the Lord.

Sally: And for the Army.

Peter: And people.

Sally: 'Barnardos' no longer have 'homes' of the kind their founder rented for eight shillings. Residential houses have been replaced by support programmes for children and families in need.

Peter: In how many cities and centres?

Sally: Over 300 in the UK. Australia and New Zealand have similar support centres.

Peter: William Booth would have said, 'Well done, Barnardo!' Did Booth include children and young people in his mission?

Sally: In the first number of *The Little Soldier* Booth said that he relied upon the honour of the troops to see that no child was ever shut out of a meeting on account of poverty, raggedness or dirt, but that the greatest love and care should be bestowed upon the most wretched of the little ones.

Peter: Barnardo would have said, 'Well done Booth'.

Sally: We have not talked at all about Doctrine 8!

Peter: That is because we both believe it with all our hearts but I wonder if the General will one day tidy up its Elizabethanisms?

Front cover of the first Musical - design by Jim Moss

On Location
with Gowans and Larsson
in Abbey Road
The Musicals

Time passes. It is almost 40 years since *Take Over Bid.* Many of the young people who took part in that and the nine musicals which followed are now grandparents.

Their grandchildren must be forgiven for asking, 'What were the Musicals, grandpa?' Neither of the creators can remember the exact dates of any première performance of one of their musicals. However, one of them, General John Gowans does record in his autobiography *There's a Boy Here* the important part played by Colonels Hubert and Jane Boardman in the production of later musicals.

The Boardmans organised summer vocational house parties at Sunbury Court where up to 100 young people came together for Bible study, reflection and Salvationist fellowship. Hubert enthusiastically agreed to absorb rehearsals for the next Musical into the already full timetable. Every ticket for the Royal Festival Hall première had been sold before the first rehearsal on the first day. On that same day, all 100 young people had been introduced to at least one of the songs for the show and charged with enthusiasm about the project. And each and every one of them had to be auditioned before they were allowed to go to sleep!

For an authoritative summary Major Sally Storey turned to Salvationist Morvyn Finch, of Woodbridge Corps.

Morvyn is a Musicals buff who has established his own 'Musicals' website   http://www.gowans-larsson.com

1.   *Take Over Bid* First public presentation: 14 October 1967, in the Reading Town Hall.

2.   *Hosea* First public presentation: 12 November 1969, in the Lewisham Town Hall, London.

3.   *Jesus Folk* A short version presented on 10 July 1972 during the finale of the British Congress held in Wembley. The full version premièred on 25 January 1973 at the Fairfield Halls, Croydon.

4.   *Spirit!* A short version presented on 23 July 1973 in the Regent Hall, London. The full version premièred on 2 September 1974 in the Kelvin Hall, Glasgow.

5.   *Glory*! Public première: 12 July 1976 in the Royal Festival Hall, London, on the occasion of the British Congress of that year.

6.   *White Rose* Premièred on 27 June 1977 at the Royal Albert Hall, London, on the occasion of the 70th Anniversary of the Home League.

7.   *The Blood of the Lamb* Premièred on 7 July 1978 in the Wembley Auditorium, London, on the occasion of the International Congress of that year.

8.   *Son of Man* Premièred on 5 June 1983 in Pasadena, Los Angeles, on the occasion of the USA Western Territory Centennial Congress.

9.   *Man Mark II* Premièred on 21 July 1985 in Macomb, Illinois, USA, on the occasion of the International Youth Congress.

10.   *The Meeting* Premièred on Friday 29 June 1990 in the Wembley Auditorium, London, on the occasion of the International Congress of that year.

Summary prepared by Morvyn Finch
Woodbridge Corps

http://www.gowans-larsson.com

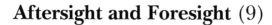

Aftersight and Foresight (9)

We believe that it is the privilege of all believers to be wholly sanctified, and that their whole spirit and soul and body may be preserved blameless unto the coming of our Lord Jesus Christ …

Doctrine 10

SALLY: The General has written, 'Just as God comes to an individual believer to break and melt and mould and fill, so he comes to groups of believers. I believe he can do this afresh for the whole international Salvation Army'.

Peter: Isn't that what Pentecost was about – the Holy Spirit coming with power into the lives of that early-day group of believers?

Sally: The experience can be renewed. 'We want another Pentecost send the fire!' as we sang last Sunday.

Theologically that is not possible. God who is spirit made himself known as the spirit of power and fire at Pentecost once and for all time. But God's people need often to recover the truth. The late Dr. Alec Vidler wrote:

> In the New Testament, the presence and life of the spirit are a corporate experience – a shared experience. No individual can recapture that experience by himself or for himself.

Peter: True in Jerusalem for those first Jewish believers.

Sally: It became true for non-Jewish believers, too, when Peter preached in the Roman fortress town of Caesarea Philippi. Perhaps Salvationist Bill Metcalf can help us to understand how a company of Christians can awake to group holiness. He quotes Dr Vidler and then asks, in an unpublished study:

Is this true?

Is the presence of the spirit a corporate experience?

If so:-

1. (a) We hold the gifts in common:-
        Romans 12:3-8; 1 Corinthians 12; Ephesians 4:7-13; 1 Peter 4:8-11

    (b) We share activity:-
        Acts 4:8; 6:3; 8:28-29.

    (c) We hold the fruit in common
        Galatians 5:22-25; Colossians 3:12

If we accept (c), we need a new view of personal holiness. It is usually taken to be a search for inner purity (1 Thessalonians 4:3; 5:23) but another look at Scripture could see it as —

2. (a) Forgiveness of others
        Matthew 6:12-15; Ephesians 4:32; Colossians 3:13; James 2:13

    (b) Non-judgement of others
        Matthew 7:1-2; Romans 14:13-15

    (c) Mutual love, which is declared to be perfection by Jesus
        John 13:34; 15:2; 1 John 3:11-12; 4:7,12,21; also Matthew 5:43-48 and 1 John 4:18

Thinking along group lines, not those of personal fulfilment, suggests other lines of study, about:

A.   UNITY

Seeking group harmony seemed to be a priority of the early Church. Jesus prayed for it (John 17.20-23) and Paul counselled it everywhere — Romans 14:19; 15:5-6; 1 Corinthians 1:10-13; Ephesians 2:6-10; 4:3-6; Philippians 2:1-4.

> Do we make such strenuous efforts to achieve true unity?
> Does our preaching emphasise it?
> What practical differences would there be in a company which put group growth before individual growth?
> What are the obstacles to oneness?

B. GIVING AND RECEIVING

Consider what an individual may —

1. Take from the group

    (a) the strength of others' gifts (see above)

    (b) forgiveness (see above and Matthew 18:18-20)

    (c) help in time of weakness:- Galatians 6:1-2: James 5:9-20

    (d) the opportunity to love God (1 John 4:20-21)

2. Give to the group

    (a) his acceptance of others (see above and Romans 14:13; Romans 15:7)

    (b) his understanding of others (1 Corinthians 10:23-24; Philippians 2:4)

Of course, these lists are interchangeable.

> Why do we find it harder to take from a group than to give to it?
> Am I (are we) a giver or taker?
> Does it matter?
> Discuss examples of corps life in which these privileges were or were not exercised.

C. DISCIPLINE

Consider some examples of discipline within the early church — Matthew 18:15-17; 1 Corinthians 5:1-8; Philippians 4:2; 1 Timothy 3:1-13; Hebrews 12:15

Do you think:

> Group purity was then more important than the circumstances of the individual?
> We follow the advice given?
> We would be radically different in our own discipline structures if we stayed closer to these models?

Sally: The Larsson-Gowans musicals became the channel of group holiness in the Army 30 years ago.

Peter: For some Christians charismatic renewal meant being 'slain in the spirit'.

Sally: Salvationists came alive in the spirit for performers and audiences alike, everywhere.

Peter: It must have been an inspiring time. Renewal is tidal, isn't it?

Sally: William Booth abhorred performance. 'To those who sing these precious truths to the people,' he urged, 'I would say:

Sing them from your own heart. Sing with the Holy Spirit's light on every word you sing. Sing so that those who hear may think very little of you or your voice or your melody, but so as they may think much of him whose messages you sing, whose love you know and feel.

The musicals were presentations, not performances, and their inspiration flows on. *Takeover Bid* was a fun piece, young people taking over the leadership of the Army, but it was more than simply a humoresque. ALOVE vibrates with the spirit of *Takeover Bid*. ALOVE is the offspring of Take over bid!

Roots, the Salvation Army convention at Southport each May bank holiday weekend is surely ongoing from the inspiration and renewal the musicals brought. And there is another tangible bequest, the production of each musical called for an ad hoc orchestra – progenitor of today's worship bands.

Peter: But group holiness is more than large crowds and fine music, isn't it?

Sally: Whenever Christian believers who normally function separately, almost in compartments, sit down together in the spirit of 'Be still and know that God is God', such openness between individuals, honesty, and above all, love will create group holiness.

Peter: The nation's family life would profit from a little more honest acceptance of each other.

Sally: Major Libbet Booth points the way and offers this:

Pause for thought – A teaching segment

- Concerning human relationships
- Leading psychologists have identified four major problems that can cause great damage, almost invariably leading to the breakdown of relationships — nick-named by an expert practitioner, Dr. John Gottman,

  The Four Horsemen of the Apocalypse
  1. Criticism
  2. Defensiveness
  3. Contempt
  4. Stonewalling

- By comparison, or as a quantifiable rule, the best relationships are mostly built on four strong foundations nick-named

The Four Pillars of Wisdom:
  1. Knowledge
  2. Understanding
  3. Acceptance
  4. Respect

- Knowledge: the search for, and discovery of, good foundations, as without 'knowing' there cannot be understanding
- Understanding: the practising of good, clear communication, as without 'understanding' there cannot be acceptance
- Acceptance: the satisfactory resolving of conflict, as without 'acceptance' there cannot be respect
- Respect: as in knowledge, understanding, acceptance, forgiveness and love in action

  … and the greatest of these is love!

Peter: Corps, church, family, what about group holiness in the community?

Sally: The Vicar of an East London parish looked in on his Saturday night youth club. Some of the young people he recognised. They attended church, others he did not know. Both groups were getting on well together.

'My old mate the Holy Spirit is working overtime!' he said to himself.

The Holy Spirit has been called 'The Executor of the Last Will and Testament of Jesus Christ'.

Peter: I read Lord Hattersley in a recent issue of *Salvationist*. I guess not every reader was pleased. Hattersley wrote:

> Last week a middle-ranking officer of The Salvation Army, who gave up a well-paid job to devote his life to the poor, attempted to convince me that homosexuality is a mortal sin.
>
> Late at night, on the streets of one of our great cities, that man offers friendship as well as help to the most degraded and (to those of a censorious turn of mind) degenerate human beings who exist just outside the boundaries of our society. And he does what he believes to be his Christian duty without the slightest suggestion of disapproval. Yet, for much of his time, he is meeting needs that result from conduct he regards as intrinsically wicked. Civilised people do not believe that drug addiction and male prostitution offend against divine ordinance. But those who do are the men and women most willing to change the fetid bandages, replace the sodden sleeping bags and – probably most difficult of all – argue, without a trace of impatience, that the time has come for some serious medical treatment. Good works, John Wesley insisted, are no guarantee of a place in Heaven. But they are most likely to be performed by people who believe that Heaven exists.
>
> The correlation is so clear that it is impossible to doubt that faith and charity go hand in hand. Whatever the reason, believers answer the call, and not just The Salvation

Army. When I was a local councillor, the Little Sisters of the Poor – right at the other end of the theological spectrum – did the weekly washing for women in back-to-back houses who were too ill to scrub for themselves.

It ought to be possible to live a Christian life without being a Christian or, better still, to take Christianity à la carte. The Bible is so full of contradictions that we can accept or reject its moral advice according to taste. Yet men and women who, like me, cannot accept the mysteries and the miracles do not go out with The Salvation Army at night.

The only possible conclusion is that faith comes with a packet of moral imperatives that, while they do not condition the attitude of all believers, influence enough of them to make them morally superior to atheists like me. The truth may make us free. But it has not made us as admirable as the average captain in The Salvation Army'.

Sally: Corps, church, family, community – I will do my best to teach group holiness.

Peter: Can holiness be taught? I think it can be communicated – one loving heart to another. Holiness is most clearly recognised in lowliness, in lowliness of heart.

Sally: And not only in the 'holiest' — St.Luke's last, least, lost and lowest.

Peter: The lowly of heart do not see themselves to be holy.

Sally: And the rest of us are shamed out of our self-approval by what we observe in them. Paul has a pleasing picture of lowliness in first Corinthians chapter 12. 'If the foot were to say; "because I am not a hand I don't belong to the body" and if the ear were to say; "because I am not an eye I don't belong to the body"… There are many parts but one body'.

Peter: Everyone has a need to belong. A sense of belonging is vital to self-worth, which is vital to loving others, and therefore to happiness. The Army strives to make people feel they belong to the family of God. Many like myself find solace and strength through involvement in its worship and social activities, but the Army reaches out to many more people through its community welfare schemes and social services. No-one is excluded. Everyone belongs to God's family and therefore to ours.

Sally: You talk like a Commissioner, Peter.

Peter: Holiness is an ideal. A mystic possession not to be studied in a classroom, or defined in a doctrine. No-one can formularise holiness for another or teach that God is in this word but not in that. Any attempt to define holiness for other people is to dispossess your own soul of its mystery, an attempt at an understanding which the Holy Spirit himself might not recognise. God is in the still small voice and the word he speaks is suited to the heart of the individual believer. Over-confident assertions can produce discord, even argument. If Major, you tell me you rejoice in the blessing of holiness, I reply 'Amen', but I cannot claim for myself more than the spirit of a disciple in Christ's school, still learning. (By the way, I note that the word 'holiness' is nowhere found in our Doctrines). Ideas inspire, words confuse.

Sally: 'Wholly sanctified', the tenth Doctrine.

Peter: And I hope I won't be labelled a heathen for preferring the word discipleship. I will come to the discipleship meeting next Sunday in the spirit of 'What does the Spirit say to the churches?' – the question asked, I think, in the last book of the Bible.

Sally: With an urgency captured for you and me, and for every Salvationist by Generals Gowan and Larsson in their fourth musical, Spirit.

Peter: If you have ears give ear to the Spirit …

Sally: Do what the Spirit prompts you to. Keep listening, Peter.

On Location
in Linscott Road, Clapton
London
Discipleship

CLAPTON CONGRESS HALL has long since disappeared, It is now remembered with nostalgia only by Salvationist senior citizens.

> In November 1881 the London Orphan Asylum, Clapton was acquired by The Salvation Army for use as a National Training Barracks (for officers) and Congress Hall, at a cost of £15,000.00. The buildings and the alterations cost £23,000.00. By the time of the opening by the Founder on Saturday 13th May 1882 £15,000.00 had been contributed; at the first meeting a further £4,500 was raised. Soon afterwards 'The War Cry' was able to report, 'total to date from all sources £22,767.11s6p'.
>
> *History of The Salvation Army,* Vol. II p. 24,
> Robert Sandall

Gone are the days when a congregation would exit from a Good Friday afternoon meeting and immediately form a queue in order to ensure admittance to the evening meeting. No bus conductor now informs his passengers, 'Linscott Road, let us all pray!' But London architects Brady and Mallalieu happily informed Major Storey that the old Congress Hall has been granted a new life as the Clapton Portico, of which there are pictures in the colour section of this book.

You could call it a resurrection story:

> When travelling along Lower Clapton Road, a sideways glance down Linscott Road reveals a dramatic vista. Axially placed at the end of the street, incongruously surrounded by ordinary London houses, stands a giant, monumental Greek portico silhouetted against the sky.

This is the remaining fragment of The Salvation Army Congress Hall.

The Orphanage was sold at auction in 1881 and was purchased for £15,000 by The Salvation Army. The ... Congress Hall – the largest Salvation Army auditorium in the country, with seating for 3,000, was the scene for major Salvation Army occasions over the years, including the Lying in State of the Founder, William Booth, in 1912 prior to his burial at Abney Park Cemetery. The Salvation Army vacated the building in 1969 when the building was bought by the local authority for school expansion.

Situated in the grounds of the Clapton Girls School, the restoration and repair of the monument was therefore a high priority ... The structure is now known as the Clapton Portico, a new learning centre to provide information and technology for school children and young adults ... based around fully equipped IT classrooms comprising 20-25 computer workshops (with) computer inter-active white boards ... and laptop dock spaces.

(Excerpted with permission from
the brief of the architects, Brady and Mallalieu).

Aftersight and Foresight (10)

We believe that continuance in a state of salvation depends upon continued obedient faith in Christ

Doctrine 9

PETER: 'Continuance in a state of salvation' – what sort of language is that? Don't you see, Major, why your doctrines need a little revision? The language may well have been acceptable in 1882 when your Clapton Congress Hall was opened, but today?

Sally: It means going on with the Lord, Peter.

Peter: Then why not say so? You have other mysterious words too – full salvation, blessing of a clean heart, holiness, sinless perfection.

Sally: Not sinless perfection, Peter. The Army mother, Catherine Booth, nailed that one to the wall many years ago. On one of the many occasions when Mrs Booth sought to correct the error she said:

Some churchmen declared that The Salvation Army did not give its soldiers spiritual instruction. Others charged it with setting before its people too high a standard of Christian living, that Salvationists were teaching sinless perfection.

I hope you will believe that we have had more experience, and more common sense, than to hold any such dogma. We hold … that God can keep that which is committed to him, and is given up heart and soul to his work.

Peter: 'Given up heart and soul to God's work', is that full salvation? The same as the blessing of a clean heart?

Holiness? – if so I'm in! I find those other words switch-off words, contemplate-your-spiritual-navel words. One of your soldiers no longer attends meetings because of what she calls their 'excoriating introspection'.

Sally: Jesus said, 'If you abide in me … you will be my disciples'.[1]

Peter: Now that's a word I can understand. Disciple. Why not call the holiness meeting the Disciples' meeting? Discipleship can be taught. Teach us about Jesus, the Teacher supreme, Jesus, the man for others like no other man before him nor any man since.

Teach us about the people he met, the places he visited, truths he taught. The Holy Spirit would be not far away. Nicodemus introduced himself to Jesus, 'Rabbi, we know you are a teacher come from God'.[2] Let Jesus teach us, Major – Christ's teaching in our heads, the Holy Spirit's confirmation in our hearts.

I want to be a scholar in Christ's academy, Major. 'Discipleship means going on with the Lord'. Doesn't that say it all?

Sally:
(sings softly)
    He who would follow the son of man
    Must take up his daily cross;
      Must walk a lonely way, and steep,
      Must for Christ suffer loss:
    Even to Calvary the way may lead,
    'Twill call for sacrifice, for sacrifice indeed.[3]

Peter: That gets to me. Who wrote those lines?

Sally: A Salvationist named May Sandford, who became Mrs Pyke. These verses (of which that is the chorus) were set to music by Eric Ball, her cousin. He was a cadet in the Victors Session, 1927 at the time.

Christ does not compel anyone to become his disciple.

---

[1] John 15:7-9
[2] John 3:2
[3] *Musical Salvationist*, October 1927

A cross is always something we choose. Rheumatism is excruciatingly painful, but it cannot be described as 'my cross'.

Peter: Don't you agree that 'discipleship' is easier to understand than those other words – sanctification, blessing of a clean heart, full salvation, holiness: they always seem to call for explanation, the officer is at pains to explain what they don't mean: discipleship – no problem.

Sally: Discipleship easier to understand? Discipleship -no problem? You mean linguistically. Discipleship calls for

sacrifice indeed. Polish-born Janina Pladek, who is now Mrs. Major Janina Neale, living with her husband Douglas in retirement in Aberdeen (see picture left), has known sacrifice.

Her remarkable story is told in *Caught in the Crossfire* by Mary Aitchison.

Was ever a book more aptly named?

When Poland was over-run in The Second World War, Janina, a school girl whose papers to study medicine at Poznan University were cruelly dashed aside, managed to escape first from the Nazi Army and then from the opposing Russian forces. She ultimately made her way to England, and was placed in a Displaced Person's camp in the west country.

Entering a telephone kiosk one day she read the words 'Salvation Army' for the first time. Already a Christian, Janina wrote to Major Ed Newall the officer at Cirencester. He wrote by return to Janina, arranged for her to visit and to experience Salvation Army life. Janina Pladek arrived at William Booth College, as a cadet in the Peacemakers session in the summer of 1948. Last year her son, Martin, and his wife were present for the ceremony marking the Army's planting in Poland.

Peter: How about a simple re-run of doctrine 9 something like this: 'We affirm ourselves to be scholars in Christ's school, tutored daily by the Holy Spirit'?

Sally: The Clapton portico is a centre of new learning.

Peter: I'm sure William Booth would be delighted that his belovèd Congress Hall is experiencing a resurrection.

Sally: I thank God I know so many lovely people who have 'given up heart and soul to God's work', to quote Catherine Booth.

Peter: Officers like you, do you mean? Fellow disciples?

The Word on the street ...

Cartoon by Gill Cox
War Cry staff designer

Sally: I count many officers among my friends, and each of them is totally dedicated to the Lord. But not only officers.

I'm thinking, for instance, of faithful sellers of *The War Cry,* week by week.

For example, Richard Maclean has been 'selling and telling' in Northern Ireland for the past fifteen years. At weekends, he visits 15 pubs, and during the week he sells *The War Cry* among neighbours and friends.

Maureen Clark has been selling *The War Cry* in Rotherham public houses on Friday evenings intermittently since 1953, and regularly for the past 19 years. Maureen will tell you that her motivation is to speak about her Lord and her faith, and to pray with people when asked.[4]

Richard in Londonderry and Maureen in Rotherham are representative of hundreds throughout these islands who bring The Word on the street, fair weather or foul, with no question of payment for what they do.

Peter: I met Gordon and Joan Quinn, soldiers of the Sunderland Monkwearmouth corps when they visited William Booth College last October.

Sally: Throughout the year 2005 Gordon placed his business, 'Glendale Presentation and Graphics' totally behind the promotion and sales of the book, *While the Light Lingers.* He negotiated reprints, each of 100 copies, with Proprint of Peterborough, stockpiled them in his warehouse, sent promotion material to every divisional commander and corps officer in the UK, despatched orders direct. All these costs were absorbed by him. This was discipleship right enough. Result – 1300 copies sold.

Peter: I read that profits from sales topped £6,000 and were gifted to William Booth College.

Sally: Yes, indeed. Another disciple who hails from the north east is Derek Foster.

Peter: The Rt. Honourable Lord Foster of Bishop Auckland, DL, DCL.

Sally: A lifetime Salvationist who came from a poor working class family and who now sits in the Lords.

Peter: Twenty six years MP for Bishop Auckland, ten of them as Labour Party Chief Whip, elevated to the Lords in 2005.

Sally: Rt. Hon – because he is a member of the Queen's Privy Council, DL, because he is Deputy Lieutenant of his county, DCL — 'Doctor of Civil Law', conferred by

---

[4] *The War Cry* 11 February 2006

Durham University in 2005. 'Politics for a Christian,' he says, 'is … the practical implementation of William Booth's vision … the sight of people sleeping rough still cries out to us – "Go and do something" … William Booth was my kind of Christian. He got himself involved in all the social problems of his day. Prayer by itself is not enough. You need both to have any lasting impact on a world that desperately needs saving.'

Peter: The staff band at Westminster?

Sally: In 1986 Lieut-Colonel Arthur Thompson, then Public Relations Secretary, contacted the chaplain to the Speaker at the House of Commons, Rev. Canon Trevor Beeson, suggesting a carol service in the Great Hall with the International Staff Band. The chaplain conferred with Derek Foster and then secured the approval of the Speaker, the Rt. Hon. Bernard Wetherill. The ISB has led these Westminster carol services every year since.

The Speaker told Derek that he was happy to give his approval for two reasons, one, as Member for Croydon he had valued Croydon Citadel's influence in the Borough; and two, a Salvationist was running his Saville Row tailoring business. He was enthusiastic about the whole idea. Derek writes:

> The service is attended by 4-500. It is a favourite with many MPs and Peers. The Speaker reads the Bible and the Speaker's chaplain pronounces the benediction. The ISB is then taken to the Speaker's suite where the parliamentary Christian wives serve a superb buffet.

Peter: What does Lord Foster look like?

Sally: *The War Cry* reported:

> With his keen, eagle-like face, Derek bears a slight resemblance to the Founder – just add the beard and a slightly bigger nose.

Peter: I wonder what Anne, Lady Foster, Derek's wife, would have to say about those comparisons!

Sally: Commissioner Alfred Gilliard is remembered as truly a disciple of Christ. There were no strangers to Gilliard, only friends he hadn't met yet. Walking to the railway station on his way to IHQ each morning he made eye-contact with every person he passed – unless, of course, they deliberately looked away. 'Good morning', he would say — no one a stranger.

Peter: Do you think that Christians other than Salvationists give themselves heart and soul to God's work?

Sally: I read about a staff-member of Westminster School. He is a Christian with a heart for the gospel. Each morning on the train from Clapham to Westminster, seated or strap-hanging, he allows his eye to move around the crowded compartment, observing each individual face.

He reflects on what might lie beyond those eyes, that forehead — anxiety? problems at home? the fear of redundancy? a sick wife? Or, on the other hand, an exultant spirit? a questing mind? Then without moving his lips he begins to go over the words of the Lord's Prayer in his mind, on behalf of each fellow traveller.

Peter: I want to be that kind of disciple.

Sally: Me, too, as they often used to sing in the old Congress Hall:

> All my days and all my hours,
> All my will and all my powers,
> All the passion of my soul,
> Not a fragment, but the whole
> Shall be thine, dear Lord. [5]

Love for souls is The Salvation Army.

Peter: And care for people is discipleship.

Dr. Albert Schweitzer gave his whole life to Africa. In his book, *The Quest of the Historical Jesus,* Schweitzer wrote:

---

[5] *SASB* Chorus 32

He comes to us as one unknown, without a name, as of old, by the lakeside, he came to those men who knew him not. He speaks to us the same word. 'Follow me' and sets us to the task which he has to fulfil for our time. He commands and to those who obey him, whether they be wise or simple, he will reveal himself in the toils, the conflicts, the suffering which they shall pass through in his fellowship; and as an ineffable mystery they shall learn in their own experience who he is!

Peter: I am glad I have come to know who he is – the Christ of the human road, the man for others like no other man before him nor any man since.

Sally: Son of man and son of God, Peter.

Peter: 'Wholly sanctified' is not how I see discipleship. People are different from each other; their circumstances differ. Surely we make allowances for a short fuse or a peptic ulcer. An early-day Commissioner, George Jolliffe, once told a congregation, William Booth was a bad-tempered old gentleman. But think of the burdens Booth carried – and think of the quality of his discipleship!

Sally: Go on with the Lord, Peter. Prayer jog. Support the Lord's work as much as possible financially. Remember to pray for people. Remember, your mercy seat awakening was a beginning, not an end. Holiness? Sanctification? Discipleship? God is his own interpreter and he will make it plain.

Peter: Commr Helen Clifton writes (*Global Exchange*, April 2006):

As a Christian leader I ... want to see men challenged by modern holiness living and teaching'.

The word 'discipleship' seems right up to date don't you think? Modern enough?

Sally: Standing here with you on the steps of the Clapton Portico I am thinking of all of those young people who will study here in the years to come. Why don't we offer a prayer on their behalf before we go home?

Peter: Amen to that.

national Training College for S.A Officers, Denmark Hill, London, England

'Nostalgia' by the late Brigadier Will Hosty

On Location
at William Booth
College

*International Mission
Statement*

THE JOURNEY to William Booth College could not have been easier or more enjoyable. The Major and Peter walked across Blackheath. There is possibly more English history in Blackheath/Greenwich than in any other square mile of English soil. They boarded a train at Blackheath Station for Denmark Hill.

Exiting from Denmark Hill Station, Peter caught sight for the first time of the College's imposing tower. Architect Gilbert Scott was reluctant to include a tower in his drawings, but General Bramwell Booth insisted upon it. 'It should symbolise the towering figure of my father, William Booth' he urged.

The College was constructed from specially imported small-size bricks from Holland in order for the architect's detailed decorative patterns to be produced to his satisfaction.

Major David Shakespeare, Business Services Director at the College, was on hand and readily outlined for Major Storey and Peter the functioning structures of the College.

William Booth College consists of:
- The Principal's Department
- The Territorial Candidates' Unit
- School for Officer Training
- School for In-Service Training and Development (SISTAD)
- The Business Services Unit

97

School for Officer Training

CADETS' academic training is based on a two year Diploma of Higher Education in Salvation Army Officer Training validated by the University of Gloucestershire. Placements include residential weeks at social services centres and at corps, together with a ten-week placement between the first and second years. Cadets are encouraged to develop significant links with a corps local to the College for mid-week and regular Sunday involvement.

The School for Officer Training also facilitates the delivery of Open Learning Correspondence Courses.

Lieutenants'[1] training is delivered by the School for Officer Training – this involves a 'Preparing for spiritual leadership' correspondence course, and attendance at residential summer schools over a period of three years.

Flexible (non-residential) training and single spouse cadetship[2] have resulted in a creative and pragmatic approach to officer training.

The College provides a professionally-run pre-school nursery for cadets' children, and an after-school club. Primary school age children attend local schools, while some older children travel further afield to schools in Westminster and Lambeth.

A continuing feature of William Booth College is the special relationship with other European Territories. The Internationalism of The Salvation Army brings enrichment to the William Booth College community

---

[1] Lieutenants are lay Salvationists who are engaged in Spiritual ministry on a full-time basis, and who usually receive a living allowance. Lieutenants will often be engaged ministry that is similar to that of officers, but their status is not that of officers as they have not entered into a covenant and have not been commissioned and ordained as Salvation Army officers and ministers of the Gospel. *Order and Regulations for Lieutenants,* IHQ 2004

[2] Until recently married cadets were only accepted for training if both were committed to become Salvation Army officers. This has now changed, hence the term single-spouse training — Ed.

School for In-service Training and Development

SISTAD exists to support the learning and development of officers, employees and other staff, including some volunteers, fulfilling roles within the United Kingdom Territory with the Republic of Ireland.

It fulfils this role by:

1. Having ten regional learning and development officers throughout the territory, who are available to support divisional teams, corps officers and social centre staff in the area of learning and development, and who provide a programme of regional courses.
2. Providing a programme of courses at William Booth College, at Sunbury Court and at centres in Scotland to officers, employees and volunteers of The Salvation Army. The courses range from leadership development and child protection to a Bachelor of Arts degree in Pastoral Care with Psychology.
3. Providing the 'Into Officership' programme for those in their first five years of officership,
4. Providing officer support seminars such as 'Facing Change' for officers within the United Kingdom and Ireland who are changing roles and 'Managing Change' for officers coming into the territory from overseas.
5. Providing the Salvation Army Vocational Assessment Centre, which is accredited to provide Scottish and National Vocational Qualifications.
6. Supporting and monitoring officers and employees undertaking higher education courses with other education providers.

   A brochure of courses is produced annually.

SISTAD also supports and monitors officers and employees undertaking higher education courses with other education providers.

David Shakespeare, Major
Business Services Director, William Booth College

Aftersight and Foresight (11)

We believe that The Salvation Army, an International Movement, is an evangelical part of the universal church. Its message is based on the Bible. Its ministry is motivated by love for God. Its mission is to preach the Gospel of Jesus Christ and meet human needs in his name without discrimination.

International Mission Statement

Sally: This college is William Booth's dream come true – a hands-on university of humanity.

Peter: You mean, this is the intention – when degree-awarding arrangements with the Open University are in place.

Sally: No, I don't mean that at all. William Booth Memorial Training College was Booth's University of Humanity from the day its doors opened to the 'Fighters' Session of cadets in 1929.

Peter: Is that how you see it?

Sally: I most certainly do. I graduated from this university with an honours degree – the rank of lieutenant – in 1983. I do hope college staff aren't suffering from some sense of academic inferiority. There is no reason for them to do so. Salvation Army cadets are special people being equipped for a special mission in this very special foundation.

Peter: But a little more education is not a bad idea, surely?

Sally: Is the aim better education for an apostle of the burning heart or is it some kind of academic recognition – for what that is worth? I'm all for the former.

Peter: The PM's battle cry – Education! Education! Education!

Sally: Study leave is provided for in *Orders and Regulations for Officers*. When degree-level studies are scheduled here,

I am afraid that cadets of poor academic calibre like mine could feel themselves to be second class, even substandard.

Peter: Time marches on, Major. This development is inevitable, and is to be welcomed.

Sally: Always recognising that Booth's University of Humanity celebrates its 77th Anniversary this year.

Peter: And William Booth its first Chancellor!

Sally: Posthumously! Chancellor, promoted to Glory – DCL of Oxford, *honoris causa.*

Peter: And we welcome graduate cadets who recognise that to be a captain in The Salvation Army is an honour of which none is worthy.

Sally: I need no convincing of the importance of the Christian life and witness of the Salvation Army soldier. There is one ministry in Christ and every individual Christian is called to share in it. Very largely, however, it is the energy and enterprise of the Salvation Army officer which maintains the efficiency and also expands the influence of the Army. The Army is a full-time service corps which must itself be served and serviced on a full-time basis.

Peter: And I want to be a soldier in your Army. Tell me more about it.

Sally: The Army has to be built all over again in every generation. We do not have the vast resources of the Roman Catholic Church, nor the state support of the Church of England, nor the scholarship and democratic structure of the Church of Scotland. All we have ultimately is the spirit of Milner and Prentice.

Peter: Who were they?

Sally: Two hallelujah lasses who were sent by William Booth to open the work in Scotland. They arrived on 23 March

1879. Three years later the Army in Scotland could boast 22 corps, 47 officers, 880 volunteer speakers, and 1,953 soldiers. Attendances at Sunday meetings totalled over 15,000, weeknight attendances over 7000.

Peter: Is the essential spirit of the Army still alive?

Sally:
(sings, quite loudly this time)

> I'm going to the Army
> I'm going to the Army
> I'm going where the biggest blessings flow,
> I hear the big drum beating
> A-calling to the meeting,
> I've got the Army fever and I must go.

Peter: A pretty jingle, Major.

Sally: You have to feel the beat of the drum in your heart, Peter. The church bell says 'Come! Come! Come!' The Army drum says 'Fetch 'em! Fetch 'em! Fetch 'em!'

Peter: Again, an attractive slogan.

Sally: Not as easy today as in the time of Milner and Prentice. Occasionally one or two who graduate from this college as commissioned officers later throw in the towel. To quote General Coutts again:

> The collapse of a man of God can have more than one cause. The seeming failure of his ministry can break his spirit. There is no measurable standard of cost effectiveness which can be applied to his work . . .

Peter: But Salvationists have an instinct to help – outside of corps life, I mean.

Sally: When the oil depot at Buncefield went up in flames, on Sunday 11 December 2005, Salvationists of the Hemel Hempstead Corps abandoned their Sunday morning meeting and rushed to the aid of the rescue services. The Salvation Army has been dubbed 'The Fourth Rescue Agency'.

The phone rings at four in the morning in the home of Major Carolyn Read in Exeter. She jumps out of bed, her husband makes her a cup of tea and she's off to Plymouth to set up support for fire-fighters at a major incident. She is the Community Services Officer for the South West Division.

Peter: Instinctive help.

Sally: 1965 was Centenary Year for the Army. The Crystal Palace Sports Complex in South London was one venue we used, on a Saturday in June. The management were not easily persuaded to allow the Army to use their facilities. They agreed on condition we included a sports element in the day, which we did.

Some 40,000 people attended. At the end of the day the spectators' stands overflowed with litter. Aware of the reluctance shown by the management to have us, the organisers of the day resolved to clean and tidy the stands.

Peter: How could they do that?

Sally: At around 8 o' clock that evening an officer phoned the corps officers of Thornton Heath and Croydon Corps. 'Could bandsmen and others rendezvous in working clothes at the ground at 8:00 the next morning, bringing bin bags and brushes'? Thirty arrived. By 10:00am the grounds were spic and span. The Salvationists went home, washed, breakfasted, donned uniform and went to the morning meeting.

Another example — Major Muriel McClenahan was honoured by Her Majesty the Queen; appointed OBE in recognition of her service with the London Resilience Team following the July 7th bombings.

Peter: The Tsunami?

Sally: Salvationist relief teams immediately went to help, but not only from the West. Indian officers and Indonesian officers were right there too. And as we speak, in one district in Indonesia in the aftermath of the Tsunami, a compassion-in-action team of Salvationists from the USA, helped by Indonesian Salvationists is reaching out to six hundred families. Our mobile health clinics bring medical care to that stricken community which would otherwise be unavailable.

Peter: Katrina?

Sally: Alongside the Red Cross, the National Guard and the Police, American Salvationists, with more than one hundred mobile canteens, served half a million hot meals daily to some 120,000 hurricane victims, iced water, too. Major Dalton Cunningham directed this vast relief programme across the counties of Alabama, Louisiana and Mississippi.

Peter: The North Pakistan earthquake?

Sally: Our special responsibility is for four thousand families still living in tents or barracks.

Peter: And the cost of these vast operations?

Sally: Just one example, £1.8 million was contributed by The Salvation Army in the UK for reconstruction programmes following the Boxing Day 2004 tsunami.

This provided food rations for about two thousand families, the replacement of fishing boats and nets – and the repair of outboard engines — 240 catamarans, 61 plots of land and new homes and a great deal more.

Peter: 'Where's there's need, there's The Salvation Army'.

Sally: Worldwide, this diversity shows itself in the help given to millions of people every year, through 539 hostels for the homeless, 211 emergency lodges, 202 children's homes, 212 homes for the elderly, some 30 homes for the disabled, and a further 725 residential homes for various purposes; 25 general hospitals, a further 123 specialist hospitals, and 346 mobile medical clinics. We operate 1,877 schools, attended by more than half a million pupils and staffed by nearly 15,000 teachers;

107 vocational training centres and 72 colleges and universities. We run 1,480 day care centres answering all manner of needs, and 220 addiction dependency programmes. We operate hundreds of disaster rehabilitation schemes, visit over a quarter-of-a-million prisoners every year and trace more than 8,000 missing people annually. We estimate the total number of people we help every year runs into many millions.

Peter: A sizeable programme.

Sally: Take our Rotoroa Island programme in New Zealand. We have operated an alcoholic rehabilitation service there since we bought the island in 1908. Currently there are 50 clients, 40 male and 10 female.

Peter: Where is Rotoroa Island?

Sally: 27 miles out from Auckland. We have owned a number of boats through the years:

1912 – 1946:	Oranga
1945 – 1951:	Oranga II
1956 – 1958:	Lady Roberts
1958 – 1971:	Mahoe
1971 – 1998:	Kaheno
1998 -	Serenity Rotoroa

Peter: What a delightful name, that last boat.

Sally: She is a high speed catamaran. The Kaheno took 2 hours and a half for the journey, the 'Serenity' only one hour ten minutes, and you should see the dolphins rise to greet her! However, after 96 years specialised service, the Bridge Programme is transferring to Auckland, and strengthening its links with other Salvation Army rehabilitation programmes in New Zealand. Current thinking favours treatment *in situ* rather than in isolation.

Peter: Tell me more about Pakistan.

Sally: We have been in Pakistan as an Army of Salvation since 1883. There are now more than 700 centres of operation in the country. Our General and Commissioner Helen Clifton served there as Territorial Leaders for five years.

Peter: The earthquake? Tell me a little more about what the Army is doing.

Sally: IHQ at once sent an emergency relief team. Major David Wakefield and a Bromley Salvationist, Katie Baddams, were two members. David wrote:

> There is hardly a building standing between what was a structure and what might have been a road or lane.

Peter: Did the relief team have specific assignments?

Sally: Our Salvation Army trucks were detailed to distribute tents to homeless families. Our tents are a distinctive red colour.

Peter: Hands on stuff!

Sally: Katie Baddams wrote about the community spirit among the people:

> The people had lost everything but they took their allocated tent, went up to the site of their old home and got on with attempting to rebuild their lives. In a sense they had no option, but the way they did it was with dignity and honour.

Peter: And in the USA?

Sally: We have a mighty Army in America – four territorial commands based on New York, Los Angeles, Chicago and Atlanta. There are over five thousand American officers serving two thousand corps and institutions. During 2004 more than 12 million individuals were helped by Army programmes of general relief and humanitarian aid. The American public responded with two billion dollars in donations, demonstrating its trust and confidence in the Army. The Army has been voted America's favourite charity for four consecutive years.

In Philadelphia more than two thousand advisory board members and Salvationists met for the seventh National Advisory Organisation Conference – another evidence of nationwide identification with the Army.

Peter: Pretty impressive.

Sally: SAWSO (Salvation Army World Services Organisation) provided hundreds of thousands of dollars for international development last year. Without the magnificent financial aid the USA gives to our Army worldwide, IHQ would be compelled to reduce its level of support to our work in developing countries.

Peter: As your International Mission Statement has it,
> The Salvation Army, an international movement, is an evangelical part of the universal church. Its message is based on the Bible. Its ministry is motivated by love for God. Its mission is to preach the gospel of Jesus Christ and meet human needs in his name without discrimination.[1]

Sally: And officer training schools all over the world, such as William Booth College here at Denmark Hill, in London, continue to generate officer power.

Peter: Standing on the steps leading into William Booth College I can feel the spirit of the place flowing out through the doors.

Sally: Actions alone are one thing. But the quality of The Salvation Army's actions is what has driven this growth; actions backed up by thought, that tackle the root of problems as well as the symptoms; actions that are often ahead of their time; from women's rights, to the age of consent, to bail hostels in the 1960s to, more recently, the integration of drug dependency and homelessness policies, the treatment of AIDS in Africa and measures to combat global human trafficking — all over the world, there's a lot more to us than cups of tea and brass bands![1]

---

[1]Excerpted from *Testament* an IHQ information leaflet

Peter: In fact the scope of your world-wide operations is almost overwhelming. Twenty languages are used every day at International Headquarters here in London, I believe.[1]

Sally: But 175 are used across the globe. We're not an English church that happens to operate globally. We are a pure breed of internationalism in our own right, free of party politics. The diversity of expression of God's love is incredibly important to us, one of our biggest strengths, and a cause for celebration.[1]

Peter: I can see that belief in God is the source of the love that motivates this world-wide ministry. It is also the source of your strength. As an evangelical part of the universal Christian church, your message is based on the Bible, and belief in God, given expression through worship and prayer, leading to belief in human worth and human potential.[1]

Sally: This motivates our actions, which aim to change individuals, and ultimately the world, for good.[1]

Peter: And that is why I hope you will have me as one of your foot soldiers.

Sally: That is what I have been hoping to hear you say. Let us talk about that next time.

Peter: Do you remember your own commissioning clearly? In 1983, wasn't it?

Sally: Very clearly indeed. I shall remember that day in the Royal Albert Hall as long as I live. For one thing it was General Election year.

I often think of the charge which was laid upon us Heralds of Hope that night. I have managed to secure a copy of the speaker's notes of his address. His text was, 'Make your calling and election sure' (II Peter 1:10). Here, read this …

[1]Excerpted from *Testament* an IHQ information leaflet

MAKE YOUR CALLING AND ELECTION SURE.
(II Peter 1:10)

SALVATION

i. The air is full of words just now, words like programme, policy, manifesto, platform, disarmament, employment and many more. Politicians have made these words their own. They represent their best hopes, but unless these words are recognised as syllables of, as derivatives from, another word, the politicians words are at their best wistful dreams, at their worst meaningless even raucous mouthings.

ii. There is one word which belongs to the people of the cross everywhere, and to Salvationists particularly. It is the word written into the very heart of our Movement. It is the word lodged at the centre of the Gospel. It is the word 'Salvation'.

iii.   Salvation! O the joyful sound!
        What pleasure to our ears!
    A sovereign balm for every wound,
        A cordial for our fears.[2]

ALL OF HUMAN HOPE IS IN THIS WORD

i. There is no other hope for the nations of the world who make one family under God.

ii. There is no other hope for Britain, for our four nations which are one — five nations when we include our ethnic brothers and sisters living with us. There is no other hope able to flourish for longer than the span of an economic cycle, or the ability of a Parliament to maintain credibility. There is no hope other than this, able to silence a nation's fears on the one hand, or curb its hunger for political hegemony on the other.

iii   Salvation! Sing salvation,
        Was e'er so grand a theme?'[2]
    All of human hope is in this word.

---

[2] *SASB* 382

EVERYTHING OF DIVINE PROMISE IS IN THIS WORD

i. 'Jesus Christ of Nazareth …crucified…raised (by God) from the dead…the stone set at naught (by the) builders became the head of the corner. Neither is there salvation in any other: for there is none other name under heaven whereby we must be saved'.

ii That ringing testimony is a sentence taken from the first gospel open-air meeting ever conducted, recorded for us in Acts 2. Salvationists continue to make this testimony to Christ in 1983, whether as field officer, re-inforcement officer, social services officer…as musician, local officer, *War Cry* herald, soldier.

iii.   Salvation shall inspire our hearts,
         And dwell upon our tongues.[3]

Everything of Divine promise is in this word.

IT IS OF SALVATION HISTORY THAT WE ALL ARE PART
IN THE MAKING OF SALVATION HISTORY
WE ARE ALL ENGAGED

i. With unshakeable trust in the wounded, triumphant and glorified Son of God, out in front in no man's land we Salvationists maintain our thrust into the battlefield of life.

ii. Sometimes, newly-commissioned officers, you will trudge rather than thrust, reduced to walking pace. Do not lose heart at such times. Have your feet 'shod with the preparation of the gospel of peace' — that describes gum boots as well as running shoes.

iii.   Each day tramping, nightly camping
         One day nearer home.

iv. …until salvation history shall come to that fulfilment of which we read in Revelation 7: 'I beheld a great multitude which no man could number of all nations and kindreds and people…saying, 'Salvation to our God and blessing and glory and worship and thanksgiving and power and might be unto our God for ever and ever…'

It is of salvation history we all are part, and it is in the making of salvation history we are all engaged.

---

[3] *SASB* 382

THEN TOGETHER LET US PROCLAIM
SALVATION FROM THE LORD
FOR WRETCHED, DYING MEN...

i. Comrades all!

You local officers, and corps cadets, and home league members and soldiers and bandsmen and songsters and friends and adherents, who are part of this prophetic moment, salute our new officers with the dedicated service of which you are capable. It is the 'salvation banner of love' beneath which we are all enrolled.

ii. Newly-commissioned officers!

We, the local officers, corps cadets, home league members, soldiers, bandsmen, songsters, adherents and friends gathered to honour you in this great arena this afternoon look to you to lead us and to help us spell out ever more joyfully for our generation this mighty hope of 'God's great, free, full salvation...offered here and now'.

iii.
> Salvation! let the echo fly
> The spacious earth around
> While all the armies of the sky
> Conspire to raise the sound.[4]

My newly-commissioned officer comrades – 'Make your calling and election sure (II Peter 1:10).

In the words of your epilogue,
> **'To such a world God sends you,**
> **Soldiers of salvation.**
> **Heralds of Hope!'**

Peter: I pray that every cadet of this and of all future sessions may go from the William Booth College with that flame burning in their hearts.

Sally: Bye for now, WBC! Duty calls!

---

[4] *SASB* 382

111

On Location
Everywhere
The Benwell-Larsson Story

All round the world the Army chariot rolls,
All round the world the Lord is saving souls,
    All round the world our soldiers will be brave,
Around our colours we will rally,
    Wave, soldiers, wave.

SASB 775

Aftersight and Foresight (12)

We believe that the Lord Jesus Christ has, by His suffering and death, made an atonement for the whole world so that whosoever will may be saved

Doctrine 6

A SUB-BRAND for The Salvation Army could well be 'Internationalism unlimited' The staff at International Headquarters breathe deeply of this air every working day, perhaps no-one more deeply than Lieut-Colonel Miriam Frederiksen, Executive Secretary to the General and Research and Planning Secretary.

Miriam's brother, John Larsson, retiring from office with Commissioner Freda, his wife, after three and a half years international leadership as the Army's 17th General, listened as his sister recounted the twin sagas of their family tree.

The date was Thursday 29 March 2006, the occasion IHQ family prayers.

People sometimes ask me: "Where are you from?' I often say that rather than having strong links to one country only, the Larsson roots are the international Salvation Army.

Here is what I sometimes call the family tree, which reflects the international service of previous generations.

Grandparents	*Grandparents*
Commr and Mrs Alfred Benwell	*Commr and Mrs Karl Larsson*

IHQ	Sweden
Argentina	Finland
British Territory	Russia
IHQ	Czechoslovakia
Denmark	South America
France	IHQ
China	Finland
The Netherlands	Norway
	Sweden

Parents Commr and Mrs Sture Larsson

British Territory
Sweden
Denmark
Chile (w Bolivia & Peru)
Argentina (w/Uruguay &
Paraguay)
Denmark
France
Finland
Norway
IHQ (IS for Europe)

The left hand list shows the Army service of our maternal, British grandfather.

Alfred Benwell [1] was just 17 years old, working on IHQ, when he joined a group of Army pioneers in Argentina. He left with just a few days warning, and didn't come back for

---

[1] The youthful A.J. Benwell ... served without a break in the Argentine for fifteen years until 1905...The newcomers (Benwell was one of a group) were sorely handicapped by their lack of Spanish. Their hundreds of penny English song books were so much lumber. In a desperate attempt to make

fifteen years. There were no homeland furloughs then! His adventures make fascinating reading: having to pick edible scraps from a bin sent round from a hotel; threatened at gun point in a meeting; imprisoned with drunks and cattle thieves for holding an open air meeting; riding on horseback over the pampas in scorching heat; singing about Jesus with his guitar for the gauchos round camp fires ...

And then there were the rats, the floods, earthquakes and revolutions. During one such, the rebels set up position just outside the quarters. Had they not surrendered at the last minute, they would all have been blown up including the Captain, his wife and baby in the house behind them.

Karl Larsson was our Swedish grandfather, the right hand list of appointments. He pioneered the Army's first period in Russia from nearby Finland. For some precious months there was complete freedom of religion, and the whole family moved to St Petersburg.

But the Bolshevik revolution changed all that, and times of hardship, persecution and starvation followed. Our father was 12, and remembered the bits of sour bread that were their daily ration.

For a lad it was exciting, though, when police raided headquarters and their home, confiscating Karl Larsson's notes and papers. Ten years ago, when we were trying to register the Army in Russia, his papers were found in KGB files, proving that the Army had been there before!

He also pioneered the work in Czechoslovakia, moving to Prague some months ahead of his wife and children, sleeping on a couch that was too short, so he had to extend it with a chair which kept gliding away during the night.

Years later, the Benwells and the Larssons met in London for the 1934 High Council, conveniently planned to coincide

---

clear the object of their coming, one of the officers would muster a few of his best-known Spanish phrases, and, sitting in the congregation, would say: 'I a sinner'. Moving forward to the bench at the front of the platform he would kneel and say, 'I seek the Saviour!' This ritual evoked the greatest hilarity among the onlookers until, after about a week, a man rose and copied the officer's words and movements. A convert was made!'

General Frederick Coutts *No Discharge in This War*, p.126

with the wedding of their daughter and son (or was it the other way round?) — for Commissioner Benwell came from China, Commissioner Larsson from Norway.

Flora and Sture Larsson then embarked on their own international service in 8 territories plus IHQ, involving 7 different languages, the middle list. Into this international family John was born, in Sweden, and five years later a little girl came along.

Our parents spoke English at home, John and I spoke Swedish, and later Danish. It was not until we moved to Chile — when John was 11 and I was 6 — that we started answering our parents in English. For the first time, the Larsson family was speaking the same language!

There were just the four of us, as family.

After leaving Sweden, we never lived again in the same country as any other relative. The term of service in South America was 7 years, and during that period we didn't come home, or have a visit, or a phone call, for that matter.

But what we had never known we didn't miss, and those years were happy and full of good memories. When we returned from South America, John went into training here in London, linking up with the Upper Norwood Corps during homeland furlough.

The story goes that some time later the census board came across this unknown name and wondered who he was, until somebody remembered he was a cadet!

I was just 13 when John left home. From then on, apart from occasional visits, contact was by letter. Our mother was a wonderful letter-writer, and wrote faithfully once a week — and so did John, and later, so did I. We didn't live in the same country again for 32 years, and during all this time, the link was by letter through our parents. We've often said that we knew far more about each other's lives when connected by letter, than when we were all living in Bromley. (Our mother kept our letters and gave them back to us — so the first five volumes of your autobiography are already written!)

John is an extremely positive person. EVERY overseas visit has been absolutely wonderful, even to the inner family circle. Could it really always be that good? Yes, honestly!

John always sees the good in every situation, in every person. I don't ever recall hearing him say something negative about somebody else - a fact which I have learnt to appreciate as a rare gift.

This International Headquarters building is a monument to transparency. Transparency also describes John Larsson. He is the same in public, in the office, in private. The Christlikeness he has written about in books and musicals is evident in his own life. John and Freda, you are retiring at a very young age compared to Grandpa Larsson who, after keeping the Army in Europe together during the war, retired at 77! Our mother was nearly 70 when our parents retired, and she then embarked on a whole new, active life. Most of her books were written in retirement, and she started going to art classes and took up oil painting.

You have both kept yourself spiritually and physically fit, so I believe great achievements lie ahead for you too, as you continue to serve the Lord and the Army in a different capacity.

Brother of mine, may God continue to bless and use you and Freda - and thank you for all you have meant to me, and still do.

On Location
in Starbuck's
Eternal
Happiness

All people that on earth do dwell,
   Sing to the Lord with cheerful voice;
Him serve with mirth, his praise forth tell,
   Come ye before him and rejoice.

SASB 3

SALVATION ARMY OFFICERS are perpetually mobile people. The day's work begins at International and at Territorial Headquarters soon after seven every morning. Put a call through to an executive officer at eight o' clock and you are likely to be told 'Sorry, he/she is in a board meeting'.

Corps officers are on call 24/7.

One newly commissioned officer enthusiastically placed a notice in the front window of his quarters.

> # Home of the Salvation Army officer
> # Any call answered, day or night
> # (NB day-time preferred)

Peter thought it quite proper for major Sally to take a day off duty on her birthday. He took her to Starbuck's for coffee and cake.

Aftersight and Foresight (13)

We believe in the eternal happiness of the righteous

Doctrine 11

PETER: These visits to Salvation Army centres have been very interesting and helpful, Major. Starbuck's this morning is less formal.

Sally: Elevenses at Starbuck's is always enjoyable. A popular rendezvous, a restful half hour following shopping. No doctrine today, Peter, it's my birthday!

Do you know Commissioner John Swinfen? John and Norma, his wife, gave 30 years service to Africa, serving as principals of our schools at Tshelanyemba, Mazoe and Howard, latterly as territorial leaders in the Congo and finally as International Secretary for Africa. In retirement John lectures on world religions at the International College for Officers. John's sense of fun is an extra. He has written a whimsical piece about coffee: Let me read it to you.

MUSINGS ABOUT COFFEE: A PERK OF RETIREMENT

CALL MY BLUFF

COFFEE OR 'COUGH-FREE'?

Did you know that coffee is a good for a cough? We heard about this somehow recently, and found it a helpful tip. It made me wonder just how it was originally discovered, and I have looked into it by a method which blends conjecture and research. You're invited to judge its validity.

We are told that the coffee bean was probably first used for human consumption in ancient Arabia and grown near the Red Sea. They say it was chewed/sucked initially (rather like betel nut or Strepsils), then they got round to soaking it whole in water and, in due course, progressed to breaking it up by pounding and, eventually, to roasting and grinding it to a rough powder.

The Arabs moved around their area of the ancient world quite a bit as traders, and took coffee-beans with them on their journeys, first as part of their provisions and medication for the voyage and later as trade goods. Here and there enterprising residents of the places they visited recognised the beans as seeds, and tried planting them as well a chewing them. Where soil, terrain and weather were kind, little coffee plantations grew up in areas to which arab dhows had sailed and arab camels trekked, initially East Africa, parts of the Middle East and India.

The major Arabian export was, of course, Islam, and coffee tended to spread where Islam spread, then beyond. It spread Eastward and Northward, through North Africa to Spain, across the Iberian peninsula into France, and gradually around Western Europe and into Britain.

Those countries with climates not conducive to growing coffee imported it, and looked for ways of doing this as cheaply as possible. For several, this meant arranging to grow it in the tropical lands they were colonising; the Portuguese in Brazil and parts of Africa and India, the Spanish in South America and far and wide, the British and French in their African and Caribbean colonies, with the Germans and Dutch spreading it into the 'East Indies' and elsewhere. Coffee's growing popularity and bitter taste also stimulated the sugar industry.

Peter: What are the *grounds* for linking 'coffee' and 'cough'?

Sally: Commr Swinfen continues: it is suggested that, before coffee became an 'in-drink' in Britain – with its famous coffee-houses in Fleet Street and elsewhere – it was promoted by early entrepreneurs as a panacea for tickles of the throat and a clogged-up chest. The product, scorned by some as being in the 'snake-oil' category, was touted in English-speaking countries, especially the United States, under the brand name *COUGH-FREE*. But it was coffee's qualities as a stimulant, a keep-you-bright-and-awake-and-alert-through-the-night-watches-fix, that commended it in military and naval circles, where it also grew in popularity as an after-dinner drink among the officer class.

Englishmen who dressed for dinner in the outlying parts of the Empire adopted it as an essential accoutrement to civilised living, growing it for sale and export as well as for their own tables. During the 18th Century, it became *de rigueur* throughout high society.

Peter: Obviously one couldn't possibly have an upper class dining accessory entitled 'Cough-Free'.

Sally: Gradually 'Cough' changed to 'Cof', the 'r' in 'Free' was dropped, and the name elided smoothly into an acceptable new form, elegant yet redolent of exotic climes and comforts: Cough-Free: Cof-Free; Cof-Fee: 'COFFEE!'

Like all such linguistic developments, this seems to have happened progressively over time. I found no evidence that the change was in any way processed by media manipulation, a Royal Commission or an Act of Parliament as might be the case with matters of similar weight today. It is most likely that it began to *simmer* as a result of an *instant* of inspiration at a Brummel/Nash/Wilde-type soirée, and gradually *percolated* through the nation.

You may also have come across the school of thought which traces the journey of coffee and its name through Turkey and France to the western world. That Arabic KAHWA becomes the Turkish KAHVEH and then the French CAFÉ. The British, asserting their firm island independence, decide to call the product COFFEE and relegate the French name to the place where you drink it. I'm told that there are also Hindi/Urdu links.

Peter: This is plausible, and probably totally accurate. But the other is more fun.

Sally: Clear indications that, very early in its history, coffee was seen as the definitive answer to problems with throat and chest, are found in the Swahili language of Tanzania and Kenya. The East African coast was a major early trading area for Arabia, and the Swahili language, as well as much else in that region, was strongly influenced by Arabian culture and the Arabic language.

The Swahili word for 'cough' is 'KOHOA'.

The Swahili word for 'coffee' is 'KAHAWA'.

Those with linguistic interests will note the closed vowel 'o' in the malady and the open vowel 'a' in the remedy, a common feature in onomatopoeic constructions.

Peter: Wow! So what do you think? Another example of the richness of ancient herbal tradition, and our tendency to divert the blessings of nature from their original purpose?

Sally: Should Boots and the others express initiative by ditching their patent remedies and signing up with Nestlé, Maxwell House and Kenco?

Peter: Should Starbuck's open a chain of respiratory clinics?

Sally: Or do we have a cautionary tale of how thinking processes can subtly lose integrity even on issues more important than coffee?

Peter: 'Thought processes can subtly lose their integrity' – isn't that what we have been discussing these several weeks?

Sally: But no Doctrine today, Peter. Did you enjoy John Swinfen's whimsy?

Peter: Great fun. There is joy in The Salvation Army right enough. And happy birthday, Major — here are some chocolates for you!

Sally: O Peter, you shouldn't! But it's not self-denial week so I can indulge! Scrumptious. Thank you very much. Talking about joy in The Salvation Army — many years ago Lieut-Colonel George Carpenter, at that time a Cadet at the William Booth College, gave his testimony in a Thursday night meeting in the Camberwell Hall. He said, 'I have had a great deal of pleasure in my time, most of it has left a nasty taste in my mouth. It is only since I have let the Lord take control of my life that I have known joy'.

Peter: I know what he meant. Joy! Joy! Joy! There is joy in The Salvation Army.

Sally: Bandmaster Alf Springate of Gillingham Corps was one of the Lord's merry men. Each summer he served on the staff of our National Schools of Music, at Sunbury Court. Alf's humour was natural and always spontaneous.

The swimming pool at Sunbury Court became part of the facilities in the 1930s, funded by the National Fitness Council. Students for the music school arrived on a glorious July Saturday, the temperature in the 80s. Sunday morning prayers concluded, a delegation waited on Alf, 'Please can we use the swimming pool after lunch?' As it was in the days of strict Sabbath observance, Alf promised to consult with the 'authorities', the National Youth Secretary, Director of the school.

At lunch Alf made the welcome announcement. Permission had been given, 'but remember lads, it's Sunday, so please swim slowly!'

Peter: Third song in the song book eh?
> Him serve with mirth, his praise forth tell,
> Come ye before him and rejoice.

Sally: As Commissioner Will Pratt reminded us in his book, *A Funny Thing Happened on the Way . . .*!

Peter: I passed a church notice board recently, it said

ANNUAL STRAWBERRY TEA

SATURDAY NEXT, 3:00PM

ALL WELCOME

NB: DUE TO WET SUMMER,

INSTEAD OF STRAWBERRIES

PRUNES WILL BE SERVED

Sally: I saw on another church wayside pulpit.

> JESUS THE CARPENTER IS
> LOOKING FOR JOINERS
> NO PREVIOUS EXPERIENCE REQUIRED!'

Peter: I heard about one of your bandsmen who was getting married. The wedding date was arranged one evening – over coffee! – with his fiancée's family. The following day he phoned her in something of a panic: 'Darling, I'm afraid we'll need to find another date. I've been looking at my diary and I see that our Silver Wedding Anniversary would fall on band practice night!'

Sally: Here's a true story.

Graduating to the third stage of our Bridge programme in Sydney, Australia, one patient was placed in charge of the pig farm at the Army's farm colony. He thoroughly enjoyed his responsibilities, developing an affection for his charges. After three months in the programme, back in the 'Bridge Centre' in Sydney, he was present with others in Sunday worship at the centre.

The Major in charge took as the subject for her Bible message the story of the Gadarene Swine.[1] After the service the officer greeted him and asked: 'Did you enjoy the meeting?' 'Yes, Major', was the reply, 'But I'm worried about all that fine pork going to waste at more than one dollar fifty a kilo'.

There certainly is joy in The Salvation Army. General Coutts wrote in *No Continuing City,* of the 'public worship of The Salvation Army (which) is that unforced blend of reverent gladness and ordered freedom, able to lift a congregation to sit in Heavenly places'.

---

[1] Mark 5:1-13

Peter: Tell me more about Coutts's 'unforced blend of reverent gladness'.

Sally: Your coffee is getting cold, drink up.

The late Colonel Will Fenwick, (his widow, Colonel Eva Fenwick is treasurer of our Ware Corps), had a fund of stories. Here is one. As a very young officer he 'covered' one Sunday at a small corps not far from his own appointment. The corps officer was away on his honeymoon. Came the time for the announcements, the corps sergeant major came forward, cleared his throat, thanked Captain Fenwick for 'a good meeting' and then said, 'Comrades, we are looking forward to the return of our own Captain from honeymoon, with his bride, next weekend. A welcome tea to them both has been arranged for next Saturday and we hope you will all plan to be present. Tickets are on sale. Now, as you are all aware, our corps is hard-pushed financially. So we have decided to save money by using some old tickets. When you buy your ticket it *is* for the wedding tea, *not* for the visit of Wokingham band, and the date is 28 August this year not 5 May last year, and the price is sixpence, not threepence, and the time is 4.30, not 7.30.

Now I am sure I have made this quite clear. Let us come along next Saturday in good numbers to give our Captain and his bride a warm welcome'.

Peter: Marvellous, do go on. I'll order some fresh coffee.

Sally: A visiting Commissioner was conducting officers' councils in Sydney. Twenty minutes into the morning session, the Commissioner well into his stride, the door at the rear of the gallery opened noisily. A dear retired couple stood discussing where they might sit.

Peter: The Commissioner struggling to keep the ship afloat? All eyes on the late arrivals?

Sally: Spotting two empty seats on the far side of the gallery the dear comrades made their way over to them.

Peter: With every eye following them.

Sally: Right! Seated at last! Immediately (with the exasperated meeting leader now near desperation) the husband produced his hearing aid, put it in his ear — a piercing shriek resulted, heard all over the hall. Adjustment was clearly required. Ear piece removed, try again. No improvement — an even louder wail. By this time the meeting was in a state of near-collapse. With a look of disgust the dear brother removed the offending hearing aid from his uncooperative orifice, sat back and observed to his wife in a 'whisper' heard in all parts of the building,

'Let me know if he says anything worth while.'

Peter: Total collapse of the visiting Commissioner, I should think.

Sally: I'll tell you one more and then we shall need to be on our way.

Peter: About another Commissioner?

Sally: As a matter of fact yes, Harry Warren who was a dearly-loved leader of past days, promoted to Glory in 1992. His final appointments, with his beautiful Danish wife, included TC, India West; Principal, William Booth College and TC, Australia East. Harry Warren was a man of many talents yet quite self-effacing in all he did.

His 'party-piece' recitals in which he assumed the rasping, husky voice of the Founder, reciting some excerpt or other from early Army history books were a delight. He had a deep, deep voice. Even more delightful were his vocal solos, accompanying himself on his concertina. He could ring the changes from deeply devotional songs to light-hearted ballads. Our current General, and fellow-cadets of the Blood and Fire session will remember Harry singing song 375, 'I'm bound for Canaan's shore' as a rollicking sea-shanty at their farewell meeting in our Camberwell Citadel — as I say, accompanying himself on his concertina, with different chording for each of the three verses. Quite brilliant. It brought the house down.

On an earlier occasion, when paddle steamers still operated on the River Clyde, Harry was on an outing with a group of officers and their children from Glasgow, along with crowds of other people hoping to enjoy the trip to Dunoon. Thick fog came down and the steamer could not reach its destination. Out came Harry's concertina with an eclectic mixture of popular secular and one or two sacred songs, and the whole ship's company was entertained until the boat finally managed it back to Glasgow. The best outing ever, thanks to Brigadier Harry, as he then was.

Peter: Go on.

Sally: Harry was taking part in a meeting at Southend Citadel. The hall was full. His deep, strong voice rang out over the congregation, his fingers deftly providing the accompaniment. A young mother, baby in her arms, was seated in the third row from the front. Suddenly her baby awoke and began to yell. The Commissioner continued into the third verse of his song, the baby's protests growing ever louder. Unable to silence the child, the mother finally stood up, gathered her baby into her arms and made towards the exit door at the rear of the hall. Harry called after her, 'Don't leave, dear lady, the baby isn't disturbing me.' Half-way up the aisle the harassed mum looked back over her shoulder, and said 'Maybe not, but you're sure disturbing my baby!'

Peter: Humour at its best. Coutts' 'unforced blending'. The orderly disorder of Salvation Army meetings.

Sally: No-one ever went to sleep in any meeting Bill Snape (Lieut-Colonel William Snape) conducted. Bill could start a party in an empty room! His funeral service, four years ago in the William Booth College Assembly Hall was like no other I have ever attended.

Every memory of him, recalled by Major Samuel Edgar, produced guffaw after guffaw. Lieut-Colonel Snape was Divisional Commander in Ireland, 1969-1972. On one occasion he was interviewed on Dublin TV. Prior to the interview he was treated very casually. On the day before the interview he made his own way to his hotel. Then, next morning, he walked the 300 yards to the TV studio. No-one seemed at all interested in this Salvation Army man. The interviewer had not researched his brief very thoroughly:

'So, what are you, Mr Snape? What is a Divisional Commander? Is it some kind of a Bishop?' Bill replied: 'Oh, dear me no! I'm like the Cardinal'.

A car was waiting to take Bill back to his hotel at the end of the interview!

Peter: I wonder if William Booth was a humourist?

Sally: He was too serious of purpose, but he disliked straight-laced formality intensely. In an address to the Annual Conference of the Christian Mission in 1876 he urged the missioners to develop warmth of heart. He said:

> Love will make you feel. A stony-hearted preacher makes a stony-hearted people. Perhaps there is no such monstrosity in the universe as a professed representative and resemblance of Jesus Christ, who goes about his business in a cold, emotionless spirit. There is a great cry in some directions for more intellect in the pulpit; it seems to me that there is a far great necessity for more heart.
>
> If there be one character which above another God must abominate, angels weep over, and devils despise, it must be the automatical preachers who can discourse by

the hour about the love of Christ, the worth of souls, the terrors of judgement, and the sorrows of the lost, with a flinty indifference or a ranting fervour which hardly lasts the service over, and which all can see is put on for the occasion. Oh, these ministerial machines! These mechanical preachers! who are quite content if their salaries are paid and a round of meetings gone through, who are the curse of Christendom and the wholesale manufacturers of backsliders and infidels. May God deliver us from them! Brethren, whatever other gifts you have, if you are to succeed, you must have hearts, and hearts that can feel.

Peter: With a readiness to laugh at yourself sometimes, not taking yourself too seriously.

Sally: But taking my work seriously, I hope.

Peter: Major, last week, announcing the forthcoming visit of the divisional commander, you said that you were anxious for a worthy attendance. Don't ever tell us you are anxious, Major, even if you are. Say you are *confident* there will be a worthy attendance, encouraging the 'feel-good' attitude among us.

Sally: Point taken, Peter. You can help me by making the good news known. I must tell you about an incident in the Christchurch, New Zealand, Citadel one Sunday. Morning meeting concluded, people were chatting in small groups. A lad, about ten years of age singled out the leader of the meeting, a visitor for the day. He stood in front of him and said:

'That was a jolly good meeting, Colonel'

'Well, thank you,' the officer replied.

'I thought your talk was good'.

'You are kind to say so,' was the reply, slightly suspicious as ten-year-old boys don't usually comment on sermons — then:

'It's my birthday today, Colonel'

'Many happy returns, young fellow. Here is a dollar bill for a birthday boy!'

Smiling happily the lad ran off. In every part of the citadel the conversations continued. Some minutes later the same young rascal stood in front of the Colonel once again, this time in company with a smiling young girl.

'Hello again' said the Colonel.

'Colonel,' said the boy, 'This is my twin sister'.

Peter: Major, Major Sally, do you know the song coming over the air? Gracie Fields, a Lancashire lass, born in Rochdale, possessed remarkable talent. She made her first stage appearance when only seven, then her professional debut followed in 1910. One song above all others made her a star — the song we're hearing now. (Joins in the singing).

> Sally, Sally, pride of our alley
> Don't ever wander away from the alley and me
> Sally, Sally... Marry me, Sally, and happy forever I'll be
> When skies are blue, you're beguiling
> And when they're grey you're still smiling, smi-i-iling
> Sally, Sally, pride of our alley
> You're more than the whole world to me...

Sally: I think it is time we were on our way, Peter.

On Location
in Peter's Home
Peter Makes a Proposal

As she moves around her quarters, Major Sally Storey finds herself humming the tune of 'Sally, Sally, pride of our alley ...' She remembers the words of two lines of the song quite clearly:

'Marry me, Sally, and happy forever I'll be'.

Each time the tune — and those words — surface she dismisses them from her mind. She will call to see Peter in his home, an official pastoral visit, to talk to him not about that foolish lyric, but to continue their talks about doctrine, and to encourage Peter to be sworn in as a Salvation Army soldier.

A corps officer visits his (also read 'her') people in their homes because:

1.   He is interested in people as people
2.   He can learn from them
3.   He is a pastor first and an administrator second
4.   Visitation gets him out of the office and into the community
5.   The Bible will be opened in the home
6.   His visit will bring joy to shut-ins
7.   He can collect filled cartridge gift envelopes
8.   It helps him to sense any trouble brewing
9.   Because he is paid to do it
10. And if the worst comes to the worst, there is always the telephone. 'O Captain, how good to hear your voice!'

— from *While the Light Lingers*, p.222

Aftersight and Foresight (14)

I now call upon all present to witness that I enter into this covenant and sign these Articles of War of my own free will, convinced that the love of Christ, who died and now lives to save me, requires from me this devotion of my life to his service for the Salvation of the whole world; and therefore I do hereby declare my full determination, by God's help, to be a true soldier of The Salvation Army.

Articles of War

MAJOR SALLY STOREY: We have covered considerable ground in the last few weeks, Peter. I hope you have found these conversations helpful. You have certainly told it as it is.

Peter: Not boring holes in my own ship. No Black and Decker drill in my hand.

Sally: Pointing out the wrinkles in your own mother's face, perhaps?

Peter: No, just applying a little anti-wrinkle cream here and there.

Sally: You still have hang-ups on one or two doctrines?

Peter: I do. God's control of the universe, Jesus son of Mary, what resurrection means, discipleship preferred to holiness as the believer's way of following Christ.

Sally: And you still want to be enrolled as a soldier. You could be an adherent, you know.

Peter: Your adherents are all lovely people — one dear fellow says he is an 'adhesive' — but *I* 'want to be a soldier of the cross brave-hearted and true'. I remember singing that years ago.

Sally: And you think you could be a soldier despite your reservations about doctrine?

Peter: I think I would not be your one and only soldier or even officer who shares these reservations. The Army is about spirit not dogma. I cannot deny what my mind demands to be recognised.

Ideas command, words confuse.

Sally: Would you wish me to explain your reservations to the Pastoral Care Council – experienced Salvationists all of them?

Peter: I have little doubt that more than one would identify with me.

Sally: You think revision of the language of the Doctrines is needed?

Peter: I hope the General would see a little revision to be long overdue.

Sally: Any suggestions?

Peter: That would be not a little presumptuous on my part. I am not yet enrolled as a soldier.

Sally: But you wish to be. Give me some idea of what you would like to see.

Peter: To abbreviate is to clarify, to simplify is to strengthen and I would very much like to see your International Mission Statement added to the Articles of Faith in some way.

Sally: Any MP is at liberty to table a Private Member's Bill, although very rarely does such a bill reach the statute book.

Peter: In that case the MP still continues to serve as a good constituency member.

Sally: Give me some idea of what you think.

Peter: To abbreviate is to concentrate, to simplify is to clarify. I have scribbled two or three possibilities … do you really want to hear them?

Sally: Go ahead!

Peter: Here is the first, starting with 'We affirm':

1.   Our faith in one God
2.   The Bible as our guide to Christian life
3.   Jesus Christ, Saviour and Lord
4.   Our discipleship in the one universal church
5.   Life beyond life

Sally: Five doctrines rather than eleven. You have another suggestion?

Peter: I affirm:

1.   One God, source of all life, to whom all life returns
2.   One saviour, Jesus Christ light of the world
3.   The Holy Spirit the Lord and giver of life
4.   The Bible as the ultimate guide for Christian discipleship
5.   Life beyond life
6.   The Army's mission to save souls, grow saints and to serve suffering humanity

Sally: You have another?

Peter: We believe:

1.   God is the source and creator of all life
2.   Jesus Christ is the light of life
3.   The Holy Spirit is the Lord and giver of life
4.   The Bible is the primary guide to Christian discipleship
5.   In life beyond life
6.   And we accept the International Mission Statement as our personal charter

Sally: Six not eleven doctrines

Peter: For a new recruit, like me, I think these might cover the essentials. But finer minds than mine would need to look at them. Here is another possibility.

1.   I believe that when life is seen as 'amazing grace' the human spirit comes to its awakening
2.   I believe that it makes good sense to nurture this new way of living

133

3. I believe that there is instinctive kindness in human beings although not all experience spiritual awakening. In those for whom Jesus Christ becomes real, human kindness becomes active goodwill

4. I believe that all life is a mystery too precious for God to allow to run away into nothingness and we may anticipate life's ending in quietness and confidence

Sally: You have been doing your homework, Peter. Any other possibilities?

Peter: How about,

I believe:

that God is the source of all life

that Jesus Christ is the light of life

that the Holy Spirit is the Lord of life

and I receive:

the Holy Spirit to ennoble my life

the teaching of the bible as my guide in life

the hope of eternal life by faith

and I accept:

the Army's International Mission Statement as my personal charter for life

and the Army's no-alcohol, no-tobacco, no non-medically prescribed drugs ethical standards.

Sally: I'm listening, go on.

Peter: We affirm:

The Bible as the ultimate written guide to life

God our Creator, source of all life

Ourselves as disciples of Jesus Christ, the light of life

The Holy Spirit, Lord of life

God's righteous rule in life and beyond life.

Sally: Alternatives, overlapping, aren't they?

Peter: Just thinking aloud, you understand. Finer spirits than mine would need to be applied to the work of revision – and, if I may dare say so, Major, dedoctrinated minds, not only noble spirits. Only dedoctrinated or undoctrinated minds can look at doctrine objectively. But may I try one more? - a bit longer and more colloquial?

Sally: Go ahead.

Peter: We believe:

1. In one God who is eternally Spirit:
2. That we come to him using either or all of three names, as Father, as Son or as Holy Spirit
3. That the life, death and resurrection of Jesus Christ reveals God's love for all his creatures and his compassion for us when we stumble
4. That our little lives will find their completion in eternal life
5. That because it is hard for many to believe these things he calls his disciples to mission on their behalf in the spirit of Christ's Nazareth manifesto.

Sally: So when you sign your Articles of War these will be the kind of paraphrases going through your mind?

Peter: Yes, Major, and I shall be remembering also that at the Annual Conference of the Christian Mission in 1874 the following resolution was passed:

> No person will be disqualified for membership on account of minor differences in doctrine provided such did not cause dissension in the Society.

Sally: A wise General encouraged officers to use the real measure of liberty each enjoys to interpret for ourselves the spirit and purposes of the Army. He said that the further an officer advances in administrative responsibilities in the Army the smaller that area of flexibility becomes, and for the General it is non-existent!

Peter: Do I hear you saying that you are willing to accept me as a soldier, with all my hang-ups, Major Sally Storey? And by the way, will you be my wife?
Will you marry me Sally?

Sally: I thought you were never going to ask, Peter

Peter: All that I am I bring to you

Sally: All that I have I share with you. I think we should kneel and offer ourselves together to the Lord. You have a very comfortable apartment, Peter. We will need to discuss yours or mine as our married home. I shall need to talk to my divisional commander about it. Post-Gowans we can be sure of his goodwill.

Peter: You have a very comfortable home yourself, the official SA officer quarters - no gold plate, but adequate in every way. Which ever, I'm happy.

Sally: SA officers are well housed. I sometimes think that we should push the point in appealing for Candidates.

Peter: The call to officership must always be to the cross, a call to service, not a call to guaranteed comfort, Although the Army rightly cares responsibly and with love, for you officers.

Sally: I remember hearing of an officer-wife who was prepared to move out of a very beautiful official quarters for love of her husband.

Peter: How was that?

Sally: They were Captains, a number of years service under their belt. For a long time her husband had been aware that he had not made the best use of his school years. He decided to undertake a distance learning course with a correspondence college, Wolsey Hall, of Oxford. Not for one moment neglecting his officer duties, he began to peg away at what was then known as the General Certificate of Education, Ordinary Level — his 'O's' — English language English Literature, History, Maths, Religious Knowledge, five subjects.

Peter: Successfully? How long did the course take?

Sally: Three years, enjoying the stimulation of writing to — and receiving from — his Wolsey Hall tutors.

Peter: Costs?

Sally: These became part of the domestic budget - his wife was a loving, positive person and agreed to the added strain on the finances. Written examinations took place under the auspices of the University of London - another added personal cost.

Peter: Did the Captain pass the test?

Sally: Comfortably, and then went for his 'A's - Advanced Level, three subjects, History, English Literature, Latin.

Peter: Another drain on the budget.

Sally: A-Levels took another three years. Latin, from scratch, including set books, was a toughey. The Captain remembers, for instance, Annual Appeal door–knock collecting, combining pleasant greetings for each house-holder with (while he/she went to retrieve the gift envelope) a little mental revision of amo, amas, amat...

Peter: Three A-levels passed successfully?

Sally: Not without hiccup. The more closely the date of the Latin exam approached the more clearly the Captain knew that he was not ready for it by a mile. One of the set books he had yet to open! But he decided to turn up at the exam rooms in Exhibition Road, near the Royal Albert Hall nevertheless. One glance at the questions confirmed his worst fears. He hadn't a chance! After 15 minutes he gathered his pens together and made his exit.

Peter: I can see the amazed look on the faces of some of the other examinees. Phew! a genius, job done, paper written! I wonder what his wife said when he returned home an hour later.

Sally: You can be sure she was not well pleased.

Peter: Was that the end of the big adventure?

Sally: By no means. His wife insisted that he got cracking right away on the work he had not done. A year later he re-sat the exam - all three subjects passed with success.

Peter: Stickability.

Sally: But that's not the end of the story, Peter. 'O's, 'A's - what about a degree, still distance learning with Wolsey Hall?

Peter: More expenditure.

Sally: Again, they re-wrote the family budget. But unexpectedly the position showed an outside chance of easing.

Peter: How was that?

Sally: Mrs. Captain's parents lived in Birmingham. Plans were made for a week's furlough with them. There were no funds for a more expensive holiday.

Peter: A 'Weekly' once mounted a competition, first prize, one week's holiday in Birmingham, second prize, two weeks holiday in Birmingham!

Sally: Seated opposite each other in the train, the Captain's wife leaned across, copy of the *Times Educational Supplement* in hand. 'Look, read this', she invited. At Euston Station she had bought a woman's magazine to read and inadvertently picked up with it the *Times Educational Supplement*. The Captain read that the Department of Education was pleased to announce 30 Mature Student's scholarships for people who could give evidence of maintained self-education since leaving school. Successful applicants would have university fees and other costs met, and their dependents would also be given financial support.

Peter: You mean that Mrs.Captain was now opening the door even wider for her husband?

Sally: And they had a daughter, 11, and a son, 9.

Peter: And that might mean the husband absent from home during term time?

Sally: And where was home going to be, anyway? No approach had as yet been made to SA administration. There was no way of anticipating what the official response might be

Peter: His wife would be aware of all this..

Sally: The Captain received notice from the Department of Education to present himself, at the address indicated, for interview on the date shown. Three or four men in grey suits seated round a table began their questioning. If he were given an award could they be assured that a university place awaited him? The Captain had anticipated this question. He had visited Cambridge and had been assured by the Censor of Fitzwilliam House (now Fitzwilliam College) W.S. Thatcher, that he would be accepted as a member of the College.

Peter: Was the Captain wearing his Salvation Army uniform?

Sally: Most certainly. He knew that to do so could not be other than to his advantage. The Army uniform opens doors, wins respect. Three days later he received word that he was one of the fortunate 30.

Peter: Where did the Army administration enter into all this?

Sally: Exactly. Salvation Army officers are not supposed to make their own private plans and then present them tied up in ribbon to their leaders. The stiffest hurdle still lay ahead. The Captain was Youth Secretary for the newly-created Central London Division, set up by the Territorial Commander as a considered attempt on his part to sustain inner-London Salvation Army life.

Peter: The Commissioner could not be expected to show a great deal of enthusiasm for a request for leave of absence, so soon after making such an important policy change and appointments.

Sally: He was not well pleased. The Captain was summoned to his office, where, too, sat the Chief Secretary, Colonel

George Grattan. The atmosphere was less than cordial as the Captain presented his case. The Commissioner was unconvinced, reminding the Captain of the achievements of past days when no such academic fripperies (he would have been too courteous to use that word) were thought desirable. With not a little temerity the Captain suggested that the Commissioner was looking back 40 years while he was looking forward 40 years.

Peter: And?

Sally: The Commissioner urged him to withdraw the request for leave of absence. Permission could not be given, 'and if you persist in this idea I shall have no alternative but to send for your papers and finalise your case'. With even greater temerity the fearful Captain replied, 'Then you must do that, Commissioner. I have no power to stop you. But *you* will do it. *I* will not do it. I will not resign my commission.' End of interview.

Peter: What happened after that?

Sally: Some days later a letter came from the Chief Secretary summarising the interview. 'You will, of course, understand that we shall need to appoint a successor as Youth Secretary, and we are asking you therefore to vacate your quarters by such and such a date.'

Peter: Inevitable I suppose.

Sally: Perfectly reasonable once the painful decision had been made that application for leave of absence could not be granted. The Administration could do no other.

Peter: So what was the family to do?

Sally: With no money the only course open was to apply for rented council housing.

Peter: With what result?

Sally: Bromley Council owned 'Halfway House' — a large mansion sub-divided into small apartments as temporary provision for homeless families pending permanent housing. Two rooms had been allocated, one sitting/bedroom, one bedroom. Facilities would be on a shared basis with other residents.

Peter: Two rooms only, man and wife, two children?

Sally: So it had to be. Should the Captain rethink? Was he asking too much of his family? His wife said, 'If you feel that this is something you must do, then I'll go along with you'.

Peter: What strength!

Sally: Imagine that 'farewell clean'! Number 27, Bishops Avenue Bromley is a lovely house. Only Salvation Army officers, perhaps officer-wives especially, know what is involved in a 'farewell clean'. As Mrs. Captain, on her knees, final duster in hand, moved backwards towards the street door, on that last morning of residence, did she, I wonder, find herself asking, 'I hope that husband of mine knows what he is asking of the children and me.'

Peter: So - into Halfway House, with no knowledge as to length of stay, how long before a rented Council property would become available.

Sally: Which would then require furnishing - for the family was moving out from a fully furnished home - furniture not theirs to take with them, the property of the Army.

Peter: For how long did this continue?

Sally: A happy ending came suddenly and unexpectedly. A letter signed by Captain John Lewis, ADC to the General, dropped through the (communal) street door.

> General Orsborn wishes to see you in his office at 11 o'clock on such-and-such a date. Please acknowledge.

Peter: A further wigging?

Sally: The Captain duly made his way to Denmark Hill, still temporary home in 1953 for IHQ since the destruction of 101 during the blitz of May 1941. Lewis ushered the Captain into the General's office.

Peter: Storm clouds?

Sally: The General greeted his interviewee with a handshake and a smile. 'What's all this I hear about you, Captain?' The Captain knew the General would have been fully briefed. Little would be needed in further presentation. The General said, 'You are a pioneer and pioneers get eaten by tigers — and what position would I be in if a hundred officers asked for what you are asking?'

Peter: What did the Captain say to that?

Sally: He replied, 'With the utmost respect, General, I would say that you would be in a very fortunate position.' Then the General fell silent, looking across the room, as though to view through the windows days long past. 'I did not have the chance of a university education when I was young,' he mused.

Peter: The Captain must have known that he was home and dry!

Sally: And he went on, 'Do you know you've been spoiling my holiday? Do you know your wife has written to my wife suggesting the administration must be crazy to refuse her husband the chance to improve himself for no other purpose than to be a better officer?'

'No, General, my wife did not tell me.'

'Mrs Orsborn, then Chief Side Officer at the College, knew your wife as a cadet. Seated in a deck chair, looking out to sea, she kept asking, "What *will* you do about that Captain?" Well, you can go to Cambridge! I fear you may not stay with us ... It's a great big world out there. You may find it too attractive. We'll have to take a chance on that. Now let us kneel and commend the whole thing to the Lord in a few moments of prayer.'

Peter: A magnanimous man.

Sally: Earlier he had asked, 'Where will you live?' The Captain explained about Halfway House. 'That can't be very comfortable' replied the General. Then, with a handshake at his office door, he added, 'Slip in to see

Colonel Ware on your way out. He may have something to tell you.' As the Captain knocked on the colonel's door, he heard — 'Yes, General, I understand General. Happy to do that General.' Then, 'Ah, Captain, happy to see you! That was the General instructing me to find a furnished quarters for you on an official basis. Indeed, we've a quarters vacant in Sirdar Road, North London. Here is the key. Make a visit, let me know what furniture you will need to fit it out throughout.'

Peter: All's well that ends well.

Sally: The saga was not yet complete. One further development. Colonel Catherine Baird, Literary Secretary at IHQ, knew Mrs. Captain's worth. The Colonel arranged for her to be appointed to the department as Secretary to Colonel Francis Evans, then Editor, *The Officer*. That happy arrangement continued until the arrival of a third child, in March 1955. However, when the Captain visited his wife in The Mother's Hospital, Clapton, just an hour before the birth, he found her sitting up in bed checking proof pages for the next issue of *The Officer*.

Peter: What a lady! And did the Captain graduate?

Sally: He would tell you that it was hard work, for he makes no claim to scholarship. 'Average common sense' he says. Fitzwilliam College days were happy days, now far in the past, although he has friends on the Faculty. It all seemed very important at the time, not so very much now. And if you were to ask him the name of his alma mater he would undoubtedly answer, 'William Booth College, Denmark Hill.'

Peter: After Cambridge?

Sally: On a Thursday morning in September 1956 the family were on their way by train to Plymouth, the Captain and his wife to the glad leadership of the Devonport Morice Town Corps. And there is one other thing.

Peter: What is that?

Sally: *Orders and Regulations for Officers* now provides for study leave, page 141. Oh, and I forgot to tell you. The first thing Mrs. Captain did on arrival in Birmingham on furlough was to go to the W. H. Smith kiosk to pay for the copy of the *Times Educational Supplement* she had inadvertently picked up at Euston and had not paid for.

Peter: A fascinating glimpse into past days. I don't know about the captain, but I would have no hesitation in saying that Mrs Captain enjoyed the blessing of holiness, or of a clean heart, or of entire sanctification or whatever.

Sally: I'm sure you are right, but I am equally sure she would have hesitated to agree with you.

Peter: You've set me thinking, you know, about that captain and his wife. They must have been a splendid team.

Sally: The captain used to say that his wife was God's best gift to him. He did not deserve her, he said.

Peter: What about us? I mean, could I join you in a partnership like that? Am I too old to be a Salvation Army officer?

Sally: A candidate offering for officership who has a minimum of nine years service to give before retirement age will be assured of friendly consideration — and in your case, dear Peter, of immediate acceptance, I am confident.

Peter: And not least because of who my wife is, my dear, dear Sally.

Yes, thro' life, thro' sorrow and thro' sinning
He shall suffice us for He hath sufficed:
Christ is the end, for Christ was the beginning,
Christ the beginning, for the end is Christ

F.W.H. Meyer, *St Paul*